SPIRIT&DESTINY
SoulSecrets

EDITED BY EMILY ANDERSON

With contributions from
Eckhart Tolle, William Bloom, Deepak Chopra,
Diana Cooper, Doreen Virtue, Silja, Sarah Shurety,
Fiona Harrold, Barefoot Doctor, David Wells,
Gordon Smith and many more

First published and distributed in the United Kingdom by:
Hay House UK Ltd, 292B Kensal Rd, London W10 5BE.
Tel.: (44) 20 8962 1230; Fax: (44) 20 8962 1239. www.hayhouse.co.uk

Published and distributed in the United States of America by:
Hay House, Inc., PO Box 5100, Carlsbad, CA 92018-5100. Tel.: (1) 760
431 7695 or (800) 654 5126; Fax (1) 760 431 6948 or (800) 650 5115.
www.hayhouse.com

Published and distributed in Australia by:
Hay House Australia Ltd, 18/36 Ralph St, Alexandria NSW 2015.
Tel.: (61) 2 9669 4299; Fax: (61) 2 9669 4144. www.hayhouse.com.au

Published and distributed in the Republic of South Africa by:
Hay House SA (Pty), Ltd, PO Box 990, Witkoppen 2068.
Tel./Fax: (27) 11 706 6612. orders@psdprom.co.za

Distributed in Canada by:
Raincoast, 9050 Shaughnessy St, Vancouver, BC V6P 6E5.
Tel.: (1) 604 323 7100; Fax: (1) 604 323 2600

© Spirit&Destiny, 2006

The authors of this book do not dispense medical advice or prescribe the use of any technique as a form of treatment for physical or medical problems without the advice of a physician, either directly or indirectly. The intent of the authors is only to offer information of a general nature to help you in your quest for emotional and spiritual wellbeing. In the event you use any of the information in this book for yourself, which is your constitutional right, the authors and the publisher assume no responsibility for your actions.

09 08 07 06   5 4 3 2 1
1st printing, September 2006
A catalogue record for this book is available from the British Library.

ISBN-10 1-4019-1032-7
ISBN-13 978-1-4019-1032-7

Design: Leanne Siu
Printed and bound in Great Britain by TJ International, Padstow, Cornwall.

Contents

Preface

Many of you reading this book will already be familiar with *Spirit&Destiny* magazine, maybe as one of our many thousands of loyal readers.

Certainly we're well known by experts working within the mind, body and spirit world. But for those who have yet to experience *Spirit&Destiny*, let me provide an introduction.

Now in its fourth year, *Spirit&Destiny* has grown to be the UK's leading mind, body and spirit magazine. A bright, modern, glossy title, each month we bring our readers an exciting mix of spiritual and new-age delights, focusing on everything from astrology and holistic medicine to psychics, palmists, paganism and greener ways of living.

Just as our content is varied and diverse, so – somewhat atypically for a magazine – are our readers, coming from a huge spectrum of walks of life.

The one thing that links them all is a fascination for the spiritual. Spirituality not in a narrow, religious sense but as it encompasses a whole range of meanings; an awareness that life is about far more than the material world of our everyday, humdrum existence.

They are united in a quest for personal self-development and enlightenment, and a desire to gain better understanding of the wider reaches of our existence. And there is a growing awareness of the importance of striving to help make the world a better, kinder place to live.

So it made sense for us to go beyond the reaches of the magazine and bring to our readers and a wider audience an exclusive and valuable insight into the collective wisdom of the gurus of the 21st century.

Our main aims in *Spirit&Destiny* are to uplift, entertain, inspire and inform. And that's exactly what we hope *Soul Secrets* will do, too.

Elayne DeLaurian
Launch Editor, *Spirit&Destiny* magazine

Introduction

In the almost four years I've spent at *Spirit&Destiny* magazine, I've had the pleasure and good fortune to meet and interview many of the very best experts and leaders in the mind, body and spirit field. I've met Eckhart Tolle, Wayne Dyer, Dadi Janki, Brian Bates and Gordon Smith in person. And I've had long, lovely chats with Diana Cooper, Emma Restall Orr, Doreen Virtue, William Bloom and Fiona Harrold, among others, on the phone. I've also enjoyed the company of many more witches, pagans, psychics, mediums, faeries, angel experts, teachers and healers of various kinds.

Having written and edited countless interviews, I thought: *Wouldn't it be great to do a book collecting together words of wisdom from all the incredible and inspirational people we've featured in* Spirit&Destiny *magazine, and plenty more whom we haven't featured yet, but hope to.*

So I drew up a list of about 150 people, of varying levels of fame and fortune, whom we wanted to ask to be in it – pioneers or leaders of their fields, people with wonderful healing and teaching skills, people who are changing the world for the better.

The aim was to get a good cross-section of big names like Deepak Chopra and Barefoot Doctor, less familiar but up-and-coming experts, and *Spirit&Destiny*'s own regular contributors and columnists. Plus, we wanted to include as many esoteric traditions as possible – from angels and aura reading to alternative health and astrology – so a wide variety of viewpoints would come across, hopefully creating something for everyone who would read the book.

Over nine months I emailed, called and chased as many of these people as possible to see if they'd like to contribute – for nothing more than the kudos of being part of the definitive collection of spiritual secrets from the very best in the mind, body and spirit world. It needed to be new work from everyone, exclusively commissioned for the book, to make the content fresh and exciting. We wanted the feeling of secrets being revealed, new information and opinions readers didn't already know, but which it was important to get out into the public domain.

A good interview is all in the questioning. Ask the right questions and you get interesting, thought-provoking and sometimes profound answers. So I came up with over 20 different questions, which were tailored to each contributor depending on their expertise. I asked people to share their sun sign, first memory, stories of past lives and inspirations as well as top tips for mind-blowing meditation, healthy diets or successful spells. Some of the most interesting answers came from questions such as: what deep beliefs keep you going when things are tough?; what is your secret fantasy to make the world a better place?; and, what do you know about where the world is heading?

To keep the book varied in pace and more magazine-like in feel, I left it up to the contributors whether they answered all the questions in a Q&A style, focused on just a couple of topics or chose just one to write a longer piece on. They had a tight deadline to work to, but, in the end, over 70 people contributed, creating some unique and very special work for *Soul Secrets*.

The chapter formation grew entirely organically. I didn't want all meditations, say, to go together in one chapter and all tips in another. I wanted the various devices to be shuffled throughout the book, so you could dip in and out anywhere and read differently paced work. So the various subjects covered – stories set in the past, present and future, and health, beauty, sex etc. – would be what shaped the formation of the book.

Fortunately, as different experts' copy came in, different chapters kept appearing until I had a clear order of how everyone's work would be best presented to be not only interesting, but also beautiful in what they covered. It was exciting to get a new piece of work in and know exactly where it would slot into the running order of things. However, right up until the last pieces were submitted, new chapters were still forming.

Perhaps surprisingly, the 'Love' chapter was one of the last to materialize, but one of the most obvious for me personally. I've always believed that love is the answer to so many of life's problems, that love really can change the world, that 'Love is all you need,' as the Beatles sang.

And here, some incredible writers and thinkers say just that. In fact, it's one of the overwhelming themes of the book and such a hopeful one that you can't fail to feel better when you've read the whole collection.

It's been thrilling and encouraging to read what everyone's had to say. I've felt truly uplifted by their wonderful work, which is mostly positive and optimistic. And where it's not, it's a wake-up call to change our ways, or an explanation of how to transform the world for the better.

It's been a real honour to be witness to and responsible for everyone's honest thoughts and open-hearted emotions, for they are powerful – especially if we all take their wisdom on board and live our lives following their invaluable advice and examples. I hope you'll all get as much enjoyment as I have out of these Soul Secrets.

Thanks and love to everyone who contributed (even those who for whatever reason didn't quite make it into the final version). Big thanks to all the readers of *Spirit&Destiny*: without you, this book wouldn't have been possible. And eternal gratitude to Elayne, launch editor and creator of *Spirit&Destiny* magazine – none of this would have happened without you.

Emily Anderson
Commissioning Editor of *Spirit&Destiny* magazine and Editor of *Soul Secrets*

Contributors Directory

Jane Alexander is a journalist and writer specializing in natural health, holistic living and contemporary spirituality.

Caroline Shola Arewa is a health and success expert and author, yoga master and life coach.

Pamela J. Ball is an author and career development counsellor who uses astrology, clairvoyance, spiritual perception and dream analysis to help her clients.

Barefoot Doctor has spent almost 40 years studying and practising martial arts, yoga and meditation plus Taoism, Buddhism, Chinese medicine, acupuncture, shiatsu, craniosacral therapy, hypnotherapy, shamanism, Native American medicine, psychic development, and various spiritual paths.

Sarah Bartlett is *Spirit&Destiny*'s resident astrologer and writer, having previously been astrologer for *Elle* magazine and *The Sunday Express*.

Brian Bates is an expert on Anglo-Saxon spirituality and worldwide shamanic practices who works with tribal elders and medicine people. A professor of psychology, he teaches Shamanic Consciousness at Sussex University.

Laura Berridge is a holistic image consultant, clothing designer, colour therapist, face reader, NLP coach and healer.

William Bloom is one of the UK's most experienced teachers, healers and authors in the field of holistic living and modern spirituality, plus the director of The Holism Network.

Dawn Breslin is one of the world's leading confidence coaches and is an author who appears regularly as an expert on confidence issues for women and practical strategies for getting out of depression on GMTV with Lorraine Kelly.

Dr John Briffa is a natural health practictioner and *Spirit&Destiny's* food guru. He has written countless articles on food and health, most recently for *The Observer* and the *Daily Mail*.

Simon Brown provides consultations in Feng Shui, face reading, macrobiotics and astrology, plus healing and shiatsu treatments.

Deepak Chopra, MD, is one of the greatest pioneers of alternative medicine who continues to change the way the world views physical, mental, emotional, spiritual and social wellness.

Sonia Choquette is a psychic, healer and spiritual teacher who specializes in leading others out of the Dark Ages and into the 21st century by helping them find creative possibility and personal power.

Carina Coen is a holistic beauty therapist based in central London who incorporates oracle card reading, aromatherapy massage, skin brushing, meditation and healing into her treatments.

Diana Cooper is a much-loved angel healer and inspirational writer with books translated into 20 languages. She travels the world facilitating workshops to bring healing and inspiration to people everywhere.

Hazel Courteney is an award-winning columnist who for 15 years has written in numerous publications including the *Daily Mail* and *The Sunday Times*. Hazel is currently a columnist with *Spirit&Destiny* and lectures widely on health and spiritual issues.

Jude Currivan, PhD, is an internationally well-known scientist, sensitive, healer and cosmic geomancer, who has researched ancient wisdom, consciousness and metaphysics since childhood. She holds a PhD in Archaeology and a Masters Degree in Physics from Oxford University, specializing in cosmology and quantum physics.

Sarah Dening is a Jungian psychotherapist with a special interest in dream analysis, synchronicity and the relationship between masculine and feminine energy. During the last ten years, she has written weekly dream interpretation columns for the *Daily Mail*, *Daily Express* and *Daily Mirror*.

Dronma is a Glasgow-born Tibetan Buddhist artist, who works with medium Gordon Smith, painting people coming through from the spirit world.

Dr Wayne W. Dyer is one of the most widely known and respected people in the field of self-empowerment. A bestselling author of many self-help classics, he has a PhD in Counselling Psychotherapy and spends much of his time teaching others how to overcome obstacles to make their dreams come true.

Cassandra Eason is solitary white witch, trained Druidess and author of 70 books worldwide on magic, divination, psychic development and nature spirituality.

Chris Fleming has had paranormal and supernatural experiences since he was born, and has become sensitive to spirits and unexplained activity including ESP, empathy and precognition. He currently investigates ghostly phenomena on Living TV's *Dead Famous* with Gail Porter.

Lynne Franks is a PR businesswoman turned holistic author, broadcaster and speaker, described by the world's media as a lifestyle guru and visionary. She is the founder of SEED – Sustainable Enterprise and Economic Dynamics – a provider of women's learning programmes on economic empowerment, sustainable business practices and community leadership.

Adam Fronteras is an astrologer, tarot reader and dreams expert and author. He also runs Esoteric Entertainment, a company which specializes in providing psychic content for the media.

George David Fryer is a spiritual teacher and psychic artist who draws spirit guides, past lives and mandalas.

Alicen Geddes-Ward is a writer and Faerie Priestess who travels throughout the UK, giving workshops and lectures on Faeriecraft. She has appeared on TV and in magazines and has been described as the 'UK's leading exponent on Faeries'.

Samantha Hamilton has been astonishing people with her psychic powers since her early teens and has written for various newspapers and magazines including *Spirit&Destiny*.

Joan Hanger is one of the world's most acclaimed dreams experts with a string of celebrity clients, once including the late

Princess Diana. Joan has a monthly column in *Take A Break's Fate&Fortune* magazine where she analyses readers' dreams.

Hamilton Harris is a psychic hair and make-up artist who uses his own colour cards, regular playing cards and his intuition to give readings, and who often appears as an expert in *Spirit&Destiny* magazine.

Fiona Harrold is one of the UK's leading life coaches and an author who gives powerful advice in a direct yet friendly way to help people focus on achieving their goals and fulfilling their dreams.

Louise L. Hay, author, teacher and lecturer, founded the mind, body, spirit book publishers Hay House in 1984 to self-publish her now bestselling books *Heal Your Body* and *You Can Heal Your Life*. The latter has now sold over 30 million copies worldwide.

Tracy Higgs is a medium, psychic and Native American card reader who appears as a regular columnist in *Spirit&Destiny* and was one of the psychics for the *X Factor* TV show.

Inbaal is a witch, astrologer and tarot card reader who currently presents Sky TV's *Psychic Interactive*, *Psychic Zone* and *Good Morning Psychic*, and is resident astrologer on TalkSport radio's *The Game Show*.

Judi James is best known as a body language expert who regularly appears in *Spirit&Destiny* magazine and on television, and writes weekly columns analysing celebrity body language. She presents her own body language series on Channel Five called *Naked Celebrity*.

Dadi Janki is the Co-administrative Head of the Brahma Kumaris World Spiritual University and one of the 'Keepers of Wisdom', an eminent group of spiritual and religious leaders who advise political leaders on the spiritual dilemmas underpinning current worldwide issues of the environment and human settlement.

Pauline Kennedy is an energy and shamanic healer, Feng Shui expert and animal communicator with a regular column in *Spirit&Destiny* magazine.

Glennie Kindred is the writer of nine books on the Earth's cycles, seasonal festivals and nature's wisdom. She's also an artist, healer and workshops holder who set up the Healing Field at the Glastonbury festival in the late 1980s.

Michele Knight is a clairvoyant, astrologer and tarot card reader who appears as a regular expert in *Spirit&Destiny* magazine and on television shows including the *X Factor* and Channel Five's *Housebusters*.

Lucy Lam is a writer and astrologer who compiles the monthly horoscopes for *Take a Break's Fate&Fortune* magazine, and astrology features and Star Dates columns for *Spirit&Destiny* magazine.

Stephen Langley is *Spirit&Destiny's* popular alternative health columnist and expert. He is a registered naturopath, homeopath, acupuncturist, Doctor of Chinese medicine and medical herbalist, and has studied holistic medicine in China, India, America, Australia, Tibet and Japan.

Richard Lawrence is a meditation teacher, psychic, UFO expert and writer of books on meditation and realising your inner potential. He is the founder of the Inner Potential Centre, London.

Gina Lazenby is an ambassador for healthy living, having spent the last 15 years researching and writing about what it takes to live a healthy, nourishing and balanced life.

Leora Lightwoman has been leading tantric workshops with couples and individuals since 1995 and regularly holds her own Diamond Light Tantra workshops and holidays dedicated to exploring your sexuality and spirituality.

Robin Lown is an experienced palmist who regularly appears in *Spirit&Destiny* magazine. He has analyzed the hands of famous clients and appeared on television shows including *Big Brother's Little Brother* and *This Morning*.

Mandy Masters is a psychic, trance medium and regular columnist in *Take A Break's Fate&Fortune* magazine.

Sue Minns is a qualified past-life regression therapist, is trained in shamanic practice, and is an author and lecturer at the College of Psychic Studies, London.

Sally Morningstar is a writer and teacher of natural magic, runs an international psychic and healing consultancy from Somerset, England, and teaches worldwide through her apprenticeship scheme, workshops and magical retreats.

Leon Nacson is one of the pioneers of the self-help movement in Australia specializing in understanding dreams and dream coaching, and regularly contributes to newspaper and magazine articles, television and radio programmes.

Michael Neill is a life coach, licensed Master Trainer of NLP, radio broadcaster, writer and creative sparkplug for successful people around the world. Well-known hypnotist Paul McKenna calls Neill his secret weapon and the two are long-time collaborators in their field.

Kelfin Oberon is a mythological poet, writer, musician and storyteller, who performs at various alternative festivals and gatherings around the UK and Ireland.

Dr Susan Phoenix is an energy healer, aura photographer, intuitive and psychologist for the deaf, whose awakening came after the tragic death of her husband Ian in one of the worst peace-time military air crashes in the UK.

Penney Poyzer is *Spirit&Destiny's* eco-living expert, otherwise known as the Queen of Green, the no-nonsense presenter of BBC2's prime-time show *No Waste Like Home.*

Emma Restall Orr is a Druid Priestess, spiritual teacher, singer, poet and and bestselling author. She was Joint Chief of the British Druid Order for over a decade, before leaving to set up the Druid Network.

Jon Sandifer is an author and expert with more than 25 years' experience in the oriental healing arts – including Feng Shui, acupressure, macrobiotics, Chinese astrology, 9 Star Ki, face reading and the I Ching.

Ian John Shillito is a psychic, medium, ghosthunter and author. He has just co-written a book about West End theatre ghosts and runs the UK's first ever gay psychic circle. He appears as a ghosthunter in *Spirit&Destiny* magazine and on Living TV's *Most Haunted*.

Sarah Shurety is an internationally recognized expert in Feng Shui, the author of many Feng Shui and house-healing books and is a regular writer for *Spirit&Destiny* magazine.

Silja is *Spirit&Destiny's* resident witch and high priestess who has been sharing her spells, advice and knowledge of the Craft since the magazine's beginning in October 2002. Silja is one of *Spirit&Destiny's* most popular columnists for her down-to-earth, friendly style and effective homespun magic.

Gordon Smith is an astoundingly accurate medium and author who travels the world to demonstrate his skills to audiences and celebrities alike. He has brought comfort and healing to thousands of people.

Chuck Spezzano is a world-renowned counsellor, trainer, author, lecturer and visionary leader with a Doctorate in Psychology, 30 years of counselling experience and 26 years of psychological research and seminar leadership.

Shelley von Strunckel is best known for her intelligent and accurate astrology columns in daily, weekly and monthly publications including *The Sunday Times* and newspapers and magazines published in Europe, the Middle East, Australia and Asia, notably Hong Kong's *South China Morning Post*, the *Gulf News*, and English, French and Chinese *Vogue*.

Alla Svirinskaya is a healer and author who comes from five generations of Russian healers. Medically trained, she has a successful private healing practice in London and has appeared many times on television, radio and in the press.

Angela Tarry is qualified as a psychotherapist and colour healer and has been doing aura photography and analysis for the last 14 years at many of the country's leading exhibitions.

Gloria Thomas is a holistic health and fitness expert and author. She practises a blend of psychological medical intuition, NLP, hypnotherapy, thought-field therapy and healing for improving mental, emotional, physical and spiritual wellbeing.

Eckhart Tolle is a spiritual teacher and author of the bestselling book *The Power of Now*, widely recognized as one of the most influential spiritual books of our time and translated into over 30 languages.

Alberto Villoldo is a psychologist, medical anthropologist and shaman, plus the founder of the Four Winds Society, which provides a scientific framework through which he can pass on the ancient art of energy medicine in workshops, talks and books.

Doreen Virtue is a well-known and much-loved spiritual Doctor of Psychology and a fourth-generation metaphysician who works with the angelic, elemental and ascended-master realms in her writings and workshops.

Jayne Wallace is a clairvoyant, a spiritual and tarot teacher and a crystal, spiritual and reiki healer. She is a regular expert in *Spirit&Destiny* and has a monthly tarot column in *Take A Break's Fate&Fortune* magazine.

Becky Walsh is a medium who teaches psychic development at the College of Psychic Studies in London, has a regular radio show on London's LBC radio, and often appears in *Spirit&Destiny* magazine.

Summer Watson is a house therapist, ley line dowser and Feng Shui expert with a passion for conscious eating, intelligent fitness, natural anti-ageing, stress survival, healthy homes and managing your life force.

Wyatt Webb, a much-sought-after therapist for 20 years, is the creator and developer of The Equine Experience, a new therapy blending horse sense with common sense at a top US spa resort in Tucson, Arizona.

David Wells is an astrologer, tarot card reader and past life expert, who appears on Living TV's *Most Haunted* and other television shows, sharing his knowledge and insights. He also writes the regular horoscopes for Scotland's *The Daily Record*.

Kate West is a witch, author and mother (in no particular order). She has been a practising witch for over 25 years, has written many inspirational books on witchcraft including *The Real Witches' …* series.

Stuart Wilde is an urban mystic, a visionary and writer. Some consider him an expert on transdimensional worlds and the phenomena of the supernatural.

Perry Wood is a communication and life coach, horse whisperer and author. He holds regular workshops and appears in *Spirit&Destiny* magazine giving sound communication advice.

SECTION ONE

**PAST, PRESENT, FUTURE;
HOPES & DREAMS; BELIEFS &
INSPIRATIONS**

Eckhart Tolle

There's a true shift in consciousness happening on the planet. But at the moment, things are getting both better and worse at the same time. The madness of the old way of doing things, the old egoic consciousness, becomes intensified and accelerated. At the same time you have many people suddenly realising a new way of being and living, ultimately discovering inner peace. It's only when enough humans have found the higher dimension of inner peace that there can be outer peace. You have to find it within first, otherwise nothing can be done.

To a large extent what happens on the planet depends on what happens to the United States. Right now, there are two movements in the United States. One is that almost all the unconsciousness is coming to the surface under the current administration in Washington. It's a similar situation to the '60s when we had the Vietnam war. That was the first time that war, the madness of it all, actually came into people's living rooms through their TV screens. Many people at that time, in America, began to see how mad the collective state of consciousness is, and so there was a disidentification from the collective. That created an opening when all the spiritual truths that came from the East were explored. Suddenly people were receptive to that and a lot of spiritual truths started to come through, as seen in the hippy movement. Everybody could see that the old patterns were, to a large extent, insane.

And this is happening again, it's repeating itself. So on the one hand you have the madness of the politics and the ego, fighting wars, the collective personality thriving off negativity seen daily on our TV screens and in all media.

On the other hand you have many people waking up spiritually. The fact that so many people see the madness again on TV every evening will also wake up many more people. It's wonderful.

It's likely that our ancient ancestors were more deeply connected to life than we are now. Animals have an innate connection to life and to being; they don't create a world of problems or destroy the planet. You can see how a dog lives, how unconditionally a dog loves, how the dog celebrates life. When the dog plays around it is celebrating its utter aliveness. Animals are more deeply connected to life. Perhaps there was a time when humans were more connnected. They hadn't separated themselves from life as most modern people have.

Almost every ancient culture has a myth of a Golden Age. It's at the beginning of the Bible when humans lived in harmony. India too has a time called Golden Age. Very many cultures have this myth, so there must be some truth to it. There must have been a time when humans lived in a more peaceful stage of consciousness. But it seems as likely that this was a natural state of humans as that they knew no other time or way of existing. So they lived that way, just like animals or plants do, without really knowing it.

But then humans were destined to lose that connection, and lose themselves almost, and then, eventually, regain something that they lost. And whenever you regain something that you've lost, you regain it at a deeper level with greater consciousness. So, we can once again find that same state of peaceful connectedness with life, but it won't be the same as going back to where we were once – it'll be deeper. That's our destiny.

PAST SECRETS

Alberto Villoldo

My first distinct memory was having a near-death experience when I was two years old. I had blood poisoning that required a massive blood transfusion. But I was born in the Third World, in Cuba, where there were no blood banks, so it was hard.

As I was being treated, I remember looking at my body from the ceiling, in the company of beings that I believed to be angels, which they were. They were very comforting creatures. I thought, 'I've got to go back to my little body even though it hurts a lot,' but they were with me, making me feel better.

When I was out of my body, I remembered who I was before I was born. I could see that I occupied many bodies, covered many lives, but that I was none of those lives, none of those bodies, although there was an essense that was me.

Every time I dropped into my little body I'd forget all this, but I would have a longing for it. But whenever I was out again I would remember clearly, which made me reticent to go back into my body.

When I was finally back in my body, of course I carried on with the life of a two-year-old. But from early on I lost the fear of death.

Michael Neill

The Search for Spirit Can Begin Anywhere, at Any Time

While I have had many experiences which have led to a profound sense of spiritual presence in my life, the first and in some ways most important one happened in the most unlikely of circumstances – while onstage in a youth theatre production of the musical *West Side Story*.

Age 15, I was playing Pepe, one of the Puerto Rican gang members. The show had already been on for several weeks, and we were beginning to hit our stride. It was hard work, lots of fun, and relatively uneventful.

There's a musical number fairly early on in the show called 'The Dance at the Gym'. It's the first chance we Puerto Ricans really get to strut our stuff. The choreography was sexy, very Latin, and it was noisy – lots of shouting of 'Ay, Carumba' and 'Chee Chee Chee' and other approximations of what a bunch of small-town white kids imagined Puerto Rican gang members would say.

This was my favourite part of the show, and this night we really got into it. We danced until the sweat was pouring, and the lights were hot and the girls were hot and the music was hot and it felt like the whole theatre was burning up. And we're all riding that passion and feeling those really intense feelings, and then we get into the scene called 'The Rumble'.

Well, we'd done this dozens of times before. The Americans taunt us, we taunt them, there's a lot of macho dancing (this time with switchblades), and, in the end, Bernardo stabs Riff and we all run like hell. Only this time, something different happened.

One of the American gang members, a big blond guy named Snowball, is looking at me and he starts calling out 'Ay, Carumba' and 'Chee Chee Chee' and making fun of the way we'd been dancing in the previous scene. And all of a sudden I went from hot to furious. Not pretend, not acting – genuinely furious.

I don't know if you've ever been insulted for your race or your colour or your religion, but I wanted to kill this guy. And the thing is, even though we were in the middle of a play, I went blind with rage.

Fortunately, just as I start to make a move towards him, part of me floats out of my body, looks at what's happening and says, 'Well, isn't this interesting? You're not really Puerto Rican. You're just pretending to be. But the anger seems real enough. Hmmm ...'

'You already know you're not your body,' the part of me continued. 'After all, you can completely change the way you look with costume and makeup. And you're not your accent, and you're certainly not your personality – that's the whole reason you enjoy acting so much, getting to try on and discard personalities without having to suffer the consequences of actually living that way.'

At this point, the play had moved on and my body began to move with it, taking itself through the choreography as it had nearly a hundred times before in rehearsal and performance. Meanwhile, the part of me that was witnessing it all from outside my body was getting on a bit of a roll.

'And apparently, if you "make believe" something long enough (like being Puerto Rican), you can even change what's sacred to you. Otherwise you would never have gotten upset at being teased for being Puerto Rican. (Let's face it – assuming you're not one, if someone called you a 'stupid tuna fish', you probably wouldn't take it personally.)'

'So if you're not your body, and you're not your emotions, and you're not your personality or what you believe to be important – who (or what) are you?'

And with that question, that curious part of me slammed back into my body and my long, rewarding and ongoing search for answers about life, the universe and everything began ...

Becky Walsh

I discovered I had strong psychic abilities when other people found me strange. I didn't think having these abilities was strange because it was all I knew; I thought everyone was the same as me.

The most prominent memory was when I was at a sleep-over at a friend's house, when I was about seven years old. I could tell my friend's mum was upset and worrying about her marriage. So, while she was washing up I started to talk to her and ended up what's known as channeling – connecting to a higher source – and I gave her advice.

She didn't say anything. She just put me in my coat – I was still in my pyjamas – and took me home. At my front door, she told my mum she didn't want me playing with her daughter any more because I was *'spooky'*.

I realized then that it's often wise to keep my mouth shut. After that I didn't use my psychic skills until I was at secondary school. There we had blocks of classrooms and I used to use my psychic skills to find where the boys I had a crush on were!

Fiona Harrold

I love helping people improve their lives. I've been life coaching for nearly 20 years, except that it's probably been forever because my dad was a self-improvement fanatic. He was a door-to-door salesman and, like all brilliant salesmen, was an amateur psychologist and would philosophize about how to sell, how to inspire people, how to motivate people.

One of my earliest memories of this, at age 10, is of sitting in the front of the car with him, driving round Northern Ireland on a summer evening, picking up hitch-hikers and taking them wherever they were going. Little did they know that they were our guinea pigs. We'd interrogate them, find out about their lives and, more importantly, the way that they thought about their lives, the sort of perspective they had on life.

After we dropped them off we'd discuss why they were the way they were, why they had the life they had. We would make the connections between their thoughts and beliefs and the sort of life that they'd ended up with, and we would predict their future – probably remarkably accurately!

Jayne Wallace

Libra with Gemini rising

My first spiritual experience was when I was around age five or six. I was awoken by a slim lady with long dark brown hair and deep brown eyes. I felt reassurance as, somehow, I knew she was no longer alive. I felt safe and peaceful as if she was there to protect me. She was so beautiful; she had an orange glow around her and such a kind face.

'Be strong,' she said faintly.

At first I thought she was my nan, as that was the only woman I had met who had died. But this lady was too young. When I told my mum what I'd seen, she explained that I was blessed that this lady had come to visit me. She thought she may have been my guardian angel (which, later on, as I grew more awakened, I found out was true, when a medium confirmed it).

I called her Star, because she was my guiding star when I needed strength and inspiration. She visited me a lot when I was young; she was like my best friend. She taught me about people and their lives, showed me how to see their auras and helped me to link into their emotions. I began to sense the pain in others, whether it was on an emotional or psychical level, and would give people messages of help and comfort.

I also felt that she was giving me messages about my own life. She kept reassuring me about pain and suffering I would have to face in my future.

Meanwhile, my mum, who had psychic powers before me, opened my eyes to the wonderful world of spiritualism and inspired me to develop my gift, which I still enjoy using and and developing every day, and hope to continue doing till I'm old and grey.

Then, when I was 12 years old, Star came to me in my dream and whispered: 'Today you have to face all that I have prepared you for.'

Suddenly, I woke up in excruciating pain. I was so frightened, I screamed out and cried. I didn't know what was wrong. I could not have imagined pain could be so horrific. My right hip felt like it had been pulled out of its socket. I was unable to walk. No one could have ever prepared me for this next stage of my life.

My parents rushed me to hospital. I was put on traction for two weeks. Eventually, after mum suggested they test for it, I was diagnosed with juvenile rheumatoid arthritis. I went home in shock. My whole life seemed to have ended.

I spent the next four years in a deep depression, being prodded and poked in hospitals. I felt let down by Star. I pushed her to one side and lost all faith in higher energies.

But Star appeared again before I got married, at age 17. She said, 'Think before you do this.' I ignored her and went ahead with it. She was right to warn me; the marriage lasted two years.

So when she came to me and told me I was going on a wonderful journey and should move abroad, I had to trust her and go. Age 19, I headed to Tenerife to see where Star would lead me.

From the moment I left the UK, Star and I were back together once again. She helped me find my free spirit, that's deep within all of us. She showed me how to enjoy life and gave me the confidence to come out of the inner prison that I had been in for so long. From then on I listened to Star and my life has gone from pain to perfection.

• •

Barefoot Doctor

Q *Most treasured possession?*

A I don't go for favourites in any area of life any more. Your preferences shift with circumstances, so it's all relative. On a cold, dark day your house is your most treasured possession; when you want to go somewhere, your car is. So saying, one of my more treasured possessions is the gold fountain pen that belonged to my late friend and mentor, R.D. Laing.

He wrote most of his books with it, specifically *Politics Of Experience*, which totally transformed my life at the time and led to me meeting and studying with him, which in turn led to me doing everything I've done since.

Q *First memory?*

A I studied hypnotherapy and, through that, underwent extensive regression work, so I actually recall my father's sperm fertilizing my mother's ovum, the cells dividing, me growing in the womb. I distinctly recall exploring the limits of the uterus, compressing my head through the birth canal and being held upside down in a cold room and smacked on the bum to make me cry and draw breath. Then the picture skips to being in my cot, bored out of my mind and hungry.

• •

Alicen Geddes-Ward

I have quite a few memories from when I was about two years old and I do not know which is the *first*. However, I do recall a memory that is certainly the clearest in my mind and the most profound at that age …

I was at home with my mum and I was 'helping' her to dust one of the bedrooms. I remember my mum and I chatting away and it was a very dark day and raining outside. I could not reach the windowsill with my duster, so I climbed onto the bed to reach. All of a sudden I slipped between two beds that were wedged next to one another. It seemed as if I was falling like Alice in Wonderland for ages and it felt as if I had slipped into another world, a place not of our world. I remember nothing of this place, except that I was gone for a long time; an unnatural length of time. I *knew* that I had visited another place that did not belong to our reality.

Then I heard my mum asking me if I was all right and I looked up and I was climbing back up and into reality again and everything in the bedroom was familiar. I looked over my shoulder at my mum and I started to feel confused and I think that I began to cry at the relief of being back with her. Even at the age of two, that moment became profound. I knew that it was significant and not a *normal* occurence. I never told my mum what had happened to me; I just knew instinctively that I must keep it to myself, or be ridiculed.

Although it seemed that I had slipped down between two beds, I believe that I may have slipped down between two worlds. I did not know then, but I know now about the *lore of in-between* where you can find, accidentally or on purpose, Faerie Land or passage to the Otherworlds.

Adam Fronteras

Pisces, Leo ascendant and moon in Gemini.

I was very ill as a child, growing up in Devon and Cornwall, and constantly in hospital for asthma. When I was about six years old, my parents noted that I had a tendency to tell them if those in the beds next to mine would get better.

My interest in the paranormal began at age eight, and two years later my parents bought me a set of tarot cards. They actually didn't realize what they'd got and thought it was a variation of bridge or canasta. They were a traditional Marseilles deck with no pictures on the minor Arcana. Overnight I had learnt them by heart.

The next day, my parents came in to Great Ormond Street Hospital to hear gossip from the Spanish cleaners that I had the gift or 'eye' for the cards. When they came on the ward, there I was surrounded by nurses having their tarot cards read.

I actually now have over 200 decks of tarot cards, collected over the years, some rare. I have been interested in the history of the development of the tarot for many years. Much of what is written about the Tarot is false, made-up or even guessed.

To me the tarot images are part of our collective unconscious and, although the actual cards may not go further back than the Middle Ages, the fundamental images have been imprinted on man through the aeons. The simplicity of the tarot is that it gets to the heart of an issue.

• •

Sue Minns

I've lived in Kenya, London and Egypt and have a small place in a healing centre in Brazil. Having written three books and been involved in metaphysics and the spiritual journey ever since I can remember, I'm absolutely passionate about my work, the core of which revolves around past-life regression.

There isn't time, now, to go through years of analysis, and if you are on a spiritual path, I don't believe it's necessary. Past-life regression – or deep-memory process – has continually proved itself to me to be a powerful and empowering tool for those journeying to Self Discovery. Not only can it release us from paralysing patterns, relationships, fears, phobias and sometimes physical symptoms, but it also gives us a chance to realize and know that we are souls having human experiences. Our unfinished business – karma – from previous life dramas creates the situations, mind-sets and meetings with particular people that occur in this present life.

Part of the deal, as the soul inhabits its present form, is to forget the details of its past experiences. These are held, like our own personal websites, waiting for unfinished business to be cleared or edited by the current computer operator. There are always clues as to what needs to be addressed, remembered, healed or released. These clues are all around us.

Whenever you use the prefix, 'I don't know why but ... I don't trust people / love Victorian dramas / can't stand heights / daren't talk about what I believe,' you have a key to the story that is hidden behind the scenes. That birthmark, fear of fire, or pull to visit Outer Mongolia is a link to your personal website, as is the person you meet whom you feel you've known forever, or an intense encounter that seems as if you've entered the asteroid belt – all are links to other lifetimes.

Our souls are forever trying to get us to wake up from our sleepwalking state and release us from the concrete jackets of tribal conditioning. We are free spirits who have been through a couple of thousand years of amnesia!

And when the going gets tough, and then tougher, and when all the meditations, spiritual practices, tarot readings and crystal healings bring no respite, just remind yourself that the sky is always blue behind the storms and tornadoes, and there is always a reason for everything that happens to us, even if it's not clear when we're in the thick of it all.

We are in the middle of a Grand Karmic Clearance Sale which is taking us to a place where the soul flies free on the wings of the heart.

Leon Nacson

Q *Who were you in a past life?*

A I believe it's more about *what* we were in a past life, rather than who. Was I an Egyptian during their golden age, a Roman experiencing a decline of an empire, or a Native American Indian evolving in the most natural surroundings? I've consciously tried not to pinpoint a name, address and phone number. I've concentrated on a time, an era and the experience. More like a karmic high school: these are the experiences that are required before graduation.

Q *Most spooky experience?*

A Walking down a street in Rome, and sitting on a rock in an old temple in Egypt, and having the feeling that I've been there before. The surroundings seem familiar and there's a feeling of euphoria, yet my passport says that this is my first visit!

• •

Kate West

I'm a fairly typical Gemini, but I find that I'm most in tune with the phases of the moon; it influences my energy levels, moods and, of course, my witchcraft. From my youth I've always loved to look at the moon, and, when she is full, to bask in her radiance.

My earliest memories are of being able to run pretty

much wild and free. My mother was the live-in carer of an elderly lady who had a substantial estate. I was lucky enough to watch foxes and other wildlife in their natural habitat, and to learn about the ways of nature from living in it. From the lady who owned the house, I was able to learn some of the things I now know to be important parts of the traditional Craft – such as the knowledge that there is a 'beyond' and the ability to learn to see it, and the waxing and waning of the energies which accompany the phases of the moon.

I remember long glorious summers, and winters where the snow piled deep against the trees and around the house. Living so close to nature we sowed, tended and harvested our own vegetables, collected eggs from the hens and even selected our own chickens for the pot. I feel incredibly fortunate to have been introduced to the cycles of life at such an early age.

• •

Mandy Masters

When I was about five or six years old, if ever I felt anxious or insecure, I'd always hear a voice say, 'You'll be okay. Everyone will be okay because you're here.' So I felt reassured. I never wondered where the voice came from.

Stranger experiences came when I was 14 and went to Lourdes. My mum arranged for my younger sister and me to go with a charity which took people with disabilities to go in the holy baths.

One night, my sister and I were in the bedroom we were sharing, which had French doors. All of a sudden the doors flew open and in floated what looked like a nun, but with no face. I woke my sister up and screamed, 'Please put the light on! Someone's in our room.' But when she put the light on there was no one there. It was scary.

The following day, I made my way, on my own, down to the sacred water in the rocky grotto at Massabeille, where in 1858 Saint Bernadette had seen the vision of the Lady Mary.

Suddenly, I felt very strange. It sounds daft, but as I looked over into the water, a big fish came up and spoke to me. I can't remember what it said but I knew something was different from then on. I knew that I'd seen the spirit of a nun the night before. On top of that, bathing in the holy water completely got rid of a skin rash I'd got from my horse. It was all unbelievable.

That day, I knew that I was special. I know I'm different because I was born without arms, but I could tell I would be different beyond that. At the time though, as a teenager, I thought I was going mad. I wish I'd paid more attention and started reading tarot cards, learning and practising mediumship straight away.

It's weird because when people do readings for me they always see this nun standing behind me. I don't tell anyone about her, but they know she's there. I asked a

Romany lady, who read for me, if this nun had a name. 'Mary,' she said. And I said, 'What – *the* Mary?' 'Yes,' she said, 'and she was with you when you were born.'

• •

Judi James

I have always been visually perceptive for two key reasons: I'm an only child, so more of a 'watcher' than someone who joins in, and I am and have always been extremely shy. I was an avid thumb-sucker as a child, much happier to sit staring in silence than speaking.

My career turning point came when I went to a talk many years ago from a woman who had been through a lot of tragedy. She should have evoked pity and warmth but the audience took a total dislike to her. I pondered over this reversal for months before I put the response down to her body language. There was something about the way she held herself that appeared arrogant. That emotion got under the radar and affected the audience subconsciously, overriding any feelings of pity. It was horrible but it made me realize the impact of our non-verbal signals.

David Wells

Q *Sun sign and other planetary influences?*

A Sun Gemini, Moon Sagittarius, Scorpio Rising – Neptune conjunct ascendant.

Q *First memory?*

A Looking into my mother's eyes when I was born. This graphic image was brought to me during a past-life regression that slipped into a progression where I saw my incarnation into this life. It was a magical experience that I have never forgotten. Not only did I see my mum, I saw what happens just before you incarnate and I'm not telling what it is – you'll have to find out for yourself one day!

Q *Most treasured possession and why?*

A My father's watch. He died recently and, although we were close, I never told him enough that I loved him. Now when I hold his watch I can feel close to him. Many people think because of the work I do it's easier to accept loss, but it isn't. I guess we just handle it in a different way.

It's so important to say what you feel when you feel it, and then say it again.

Q *Spirit guide story*

A My guide is a Native American Indian; I wanted a plumber or a bricklayer! I didn't take to him at all when he came to me and I think he has found me a challenge. But we worked at it and it wasn't until I recognized him from a former life where I had been his wife, that I really understood how it works for us! He says little and I ask a lot, just like any marriage.

Build a relationship with your guide, it will make things easier when you really need their advice or want to go against it!

Q *Who were you in a past life?*

A I have seen many lives from pauper to prince and no matter what you have physically it's how you deal with others emotionally that counts.

Q *Describe a guided meditation that connects you to past lives.*

A A past-life regression can lead you to lots of different places; sometimes a past life is the last thing you get!

An easy one is to imagine you are walking through a forest.

Try to use all your senses – see it, smell it, touch it, hear it, taste and imagine it.

Walk through the forest until you are met by an animal, your animal guide.

Now follow it to a doorway made of silver.

Go through the door and into the base of an old oak tree. Sit there for a while to see who appears — or not.

Then move to the back of the room where you find another door, this time made of bronze.

Wait for the door to open and go into a corridor full of artefacts from your former lives. Look at them, remember them and keep walking up the corridor until you come to a golden door.

Walk through it and into a mist that will clear to show you the life your soul has chosen to show you. Experience it as it unfolds and when you are ready retrace your steps and bring your consciousness back into the present.

Sometimes you will see guides, sometimes you will see other magical beings — just go with whatever you get and don't analyze!

That's my biggest tip for meditations — *do not analyze* when you are in it; you can and should do that later.

PRESENT SECRETS

Tracy Higgs

Meditation miracles

After the opening meditation at my first psychic development circle, I started to feel the sensation of a beard on my face and felt as if I was wearing a hat. The leader of the circle simply told me it was my spirit guide come to meet me. But my cousin, whom I'd begged to come with me as I'd half-expected everyone to be wearing funny robes, refused to drive me home until I stopped looking like a man!

People new to meditating can be held back because they believe that their minds should become instantly and totally blank, which is not the case at all. To relax into an altered state, the conscious mind seems to have to play out a series of checks to calm itself before allowing the subconscious mind to take over. If this process is not allowed then the meditation is ceased and deemed failed. But you need to allow those last thoughts, such as, *Have I left the iron on?*, to be processed.

If meditation is purely for the self to work with spirit then I would advise sitting in the power of spirit.

To do this, sit comfortably, breathing in and out through the nose.

Visualize a column of white light in front of you and imagine stepping into it, so that it fills every part of you.

Visualize the auric field around you getting bigger, like blowing up a balloon, and extending to reach every part of the room you are sitting in.

Your intention is to sit for spirit, and they will be aware of this.

However, in your mind, encourage them to step forward and just be with them with no expectations.

This exercise is to build your power from within so you can sense changes in energy around you and therefore have a clearer sense of spirit joining you. It will bring ease of communication both ways and raise your vibration.

There's a well-known saying, which I grew up believing – smile and the world smiles with you, cry and you cry alone. Since developing my spiritual gifts, I know this saying to be false. Yes, when I smile people do smile with me, but I never cry alone. Every day I see and feel spirit, not just physically, but through their signs answering questions that I put to them. I know that we are all looked after.

Perry Wood

The benefits of regular meditation are many: there is great healing power in meditation. It helps to deal with change, trauma and difficulty in life and reconnects us with the power of the universe. Through meditation you know you are not alone and that there is a greater power out there working for your good. And by reconnecting with the universe you know you are truly helped in fulfilling your destiny. Research has proven that regular meditation reduces blood pressure, improves sleep patterns and has a beneficial influence on all sorts of illnesses ... it reduces stress, which is the precursor to most illness ... and can improve personal and professional relationships too.

Whether you believe in a particular God or guiding power, if that God or your higher self wants to speak to you, you have to be able to listen, and meditation gives you the space to do that ... Many report improved intuition, even spiritual experiences and profound dreams as they make meditation a regular daily practice. Even if we don't have half an hour to spend, just five minutes of regular practice is priceless in helping us to re-centre ourselves.

To meditate, find what suits you; listen to some quiet soothing music ... concentrate on your breathing ... focus on a candle ... imagine something peaceful ... or relax each part of the body, from head to toe. I practise a powerful form called Kriya Yoga, which was brought to the West from India by Paramahansa Yogananda, the author of the famous book *Autobiography of a Yogi*.

My horses inspire me most – because they are great teachers and mirrors, constantly reflecting back to me what I communicate externally and internally in my thoughts, feelings and beliefs. They have taught me People Whispering. I love how they are with me in their honesty and clarity, constantly teaching me to be that way with myself, with them and with other people.

One of my favourite places to go for peace and 'refreshment' is Findhorn, on the Moray Firth in Scotland. I love to join the Taize sacred singing in the nature sanctuary first thing every morning, sharing in spirit with others and starting the day with the recognition of the spiritual. Followed by a walk through the sand dunes to the beach at Findhorn, where the icy North Sea hits the beautiful sweeping sand and there are often seals fishing and playing near the shore.

● ●

Leon Nacson

Make sure meditation is effortless. It never works for me if I say, 'It's time to meditate!' or 'I better hurry up, I haven't done my meditation today.'

I can effortlessly get into a meditative state by imagining a quiet place in nature and entering a crystal cave that no other living being can access. Once inside, it contains every item that I've lost or passed on; these items give me a sense of the past. My entry gives me a sense of the present and, as I relax in my hammock, which is suspended between two palm trees, I drift off to explore the world of infinite possibilities.

• •

Fiona Harrold

I learnt Transcendental Meditation many years ago, so work with a mantra. I can meditate on a clothes line now because I've been doing it for so long.

I encourage my clients to get into the habit of taking time out every day. The busier they are, the more important it is. But I tend not to use the word meditation because busy people can run when you say that word. They think it's complicated, that they'll have to go on a course, they'll have to read a book, how will they learn if they haven't got the time?

I like to demystify it by simply saying, 'Find ten or 15 minutes where you can sit down, undisturbed by ringing phones or anything else, and take that time out for yourself. Just allow your thoughts to pass on by.'

Usually these people are very busy internally too, and they find it hard to let their mind be still. So I always encourage them to have pen and paper handy so they can jot down any persistent thoughts or insights and then let

Spirit & Destiny Soul Secrets

them go. It's true, the saying that there's nothing that can't be solved by sitting quietly in a room by yourself.

• •

Alla Svirinskaya

Various research studies have concluded that there is a link between thought process and movement of the pupils in our eyes. Once you have a new idea your pupils are likely to respond with movement. While we are thinking, our pupils continuously make micromovements with the same frequency as our thoughts. It has been suggested that this link works both ways. So, by slowing down the movement of our pupils we can slow the racing of the thoughts.

PEBBLE MEDITATION

To achieve this calming effect, sit quietly, close your eyes and, if you have one, place a lavender-scented eye pillow over them.

Breathe deeply and imagine that you have small but quite heavy pebbles on the bottom of your pupils.

These pebbles don't let your eyes move, you can't shift them at all. Soon you will notice a significant change in the pace of your thought process.

It might also make it easier to observe your still eyeballs from 'deep inside yourself', feeling the stillness inside.

Follow this meditation for ten minutes every day for two weeks. You should notice you have much better control over your thoughts by the end of it.

● ●

Gordon Smith

I had to learn to meditate to help me calm down as my life is so active. To me, meditation is something that you can do whilst you're in motion and during your daily functioning, as opposed to making a certain, special time to do it. I think it should become a part of your life that you can do any time, while doing whatever you're doing. If I were cutting hair I could be meditating just by being aware, stilling the mind and focusing on everything I'm doing. I also love to do tai chi, as that connects me to that inner stillness.

It's hard to say what makes me happiest, but I laugh a lot in my life. What makes me most contented is sitting at home in Argyle, Scotland, looking over the Gare Loch, with my two English springer spaniels, Meg and Charlie, who were bizarrely born on the same day – 8th December – eight years apart. Sadly, Charlie passed away last year, so it's just Meg and me now.

What keeps me going when things are tough is my

memories of people I've met through what I do, who have had real help from the spirit world. It tells me that my mediumship really works, so I must stick to it and believe in it, no matter how much I may doubt it. When you see the turnaround in someone's life because of what you do, it's incredible. There have been thousands now.

People overcoming adversity really inspire me. Nothing lifts me more than to see someone who has been at the pits of their life, wrangling with their soul, and then, all of a sudden, they turn their life around. It's always worth remembering how strong the human spirit can be in really hard times.

We can all imagine how the world would be a better place – taking away fear would be a good start. But the world is right where it should be, and, as long as we stay grounded and can see that, it's not so bad. The only way you can make it better is to make yourself better. But it's all okay if you see it through eyes that are okay.

I have no fear of death, so I have no fear of the world ending. It doesn't bother me. Spiritually, things go on and, if the world as we know it ends, it's another part of spiritual evolution and it's time for the physical world to disappear. I know for sure that spiritual life will continue whether this material one does or not, so if it evolves onto a higher level, then that's where it should be. It's just evolution, it's nothing to be frightened of.

Angela Tarry

There is a real spiritual awareness growing in us all, which is manifesting itself in different colours in the aura. I have seen many positive changes and we must encourage these in our thoughts, actions and behaviour.

More green is evident as we become aware of the need to respect the environment and every living thing on the planet. People are waking up to the divine energy because that is what nature is all about. Parents of babies and young children often have a lot of green in their aura, because they feel more of a need to safeguard the future of the planet for their children. Hence there is more interest in alternative therapies, nutrition and ecology.

A lighter blue than in the past is also appearing, as people get involved in different kinds of healing practices. This also suggests we are all looking for clear ways to express ourselves more openly and honestly.

The dense, dark yellow that was often seen around the head, reflecting fear and worry, is now lightening. There's a white glow at the top of the aura, which is spiritual energy wanting more expression. It's important to connect to it in quiet moments, breathing deeply and relaxing, and sending thoughts to this divine energy, waiting for recognition. The tremendous interest in angels shows that we want this connection in whatever way feels right for us.

Increasingly, I'm seeing a wonderful magenta pink around both men and women, showing how both sexes are changing and evolving. This colour reflects feminine energy, intuition and compassion. Women are wanting to express more of themselves and the qualities of woman-hood. I say, 'Honour the Goddess, be the wise woman.' Men need to acknowledge the nurturing, inspirational, feminine qualities in themselves and allow these emotional, caring aspects to be seen without embarrassment or fear of ridicule. It's becoming harder for them to keep up the old macho facade. Women can help by reassuring them that 'It's okay to feel.'

As we encourage and express these new aspects of ourselves, we grow and help restore the balance of humanity, nature and the planet. As we do this as individuals we help to lighten the vibration of the collective consciousness. Positive thought is powerful and essential – every day try to find something that makes your soul sing. This will bring a feeling of peace and wellbeing, and make your auras lighten and vibrate more radiantly.

Dronma

When I work with Gordon Smith, he stands back and lets me get the first link to the consciousness I am to draw. Then Gordon links to that consciousness, usually after the drawing is under way.

Before I start working I clear my mind and try to have no preconceptions at all. Those coming through don't show themselves; they let me feel the face for an impression. If I saw with my inner eye, I would take too long, looking, measuring, as I would as an artist.

As the face is drawn, in my own body I can feel the physical conditions of how they passed or of ailments they had. I get vivid visual flashes of places and things, too. Rarely do I get verbal information like names; that's the job of the medium I'm working with. We have no say or control over who is coming – that is up to them.

My best tip for meditation is to gently concentrate on your breathing for a while, to clear your mind. Then imagine a white light flowing gently down from the crown of your head to your heart centre, where a beautiful flower opens and gently turns clockwise. As it turns, rainbows gently flow from the petals out to the world to find people who are in need.

The light then flows from the top of their heads down into their hearts and the process repeats itself until all beings receive happiness and comfort. It's a form of healing too; as others feel healed so you yourself are healed. As you give out, more comes to you.

Barefoot Doctor

Q *What makes you happiest?*

A Doing a really powerful guided meditation, live in the 'Meditation Chamber' on my site, when there are 35 people in at once from different parts of the world. Walking down to the beach near where I live on a hot summer's day in the middle of work and taking a swim in the aqua blue water – that usually hits the spot. Doing a classic round of tai chi when I all but disappear and the tai chi does me instead. And when the Supreme Squeeze, my wife, gives me one of her 'I love you' smiles.

Q *Top tip for meditation*

A My tip is a conglomerate tip consisting of breathing slowly, evenly and quietly low down in your belly, lengthening your spine, sinking all your muscles and soft tissue towards the ground, softening your chest and finally drawing your awareness back out of your forebrain where all the internal noise goes on, into the centre of your brain instead. From there if you need any guidance, I'd say it was to get the feeling of falling backwards through space at a hypersonic pace until you feel yourself caught in the arms of the Tao, the great mother of all existence and non-existence.

Q *Secret lucky charm / ritual / mantra for good luck*

A Put out good energy to the world around you, be generous to those in your life and even those you don't know, smile at people from your heart, acknowledge people and help them feel worthwhile. That energy will make its rounds, picking up other friendly energy and eventually return to you greatly multiplied. That would be tantamount to doing some magic for good luck.

● ●

Kate West

I write guided meditations, and my favourite takes the form of a moonlit walk through ancient woodlands to a lake where I can meet and talk with one of the aspects of the Triple Goddess. I often use it myself when I have a question or want to make sure I am headed in the right direction.

MEDITATION TO MEET THE
TRIPLE GODDESS

This meditation can be read by one person to another or to a group. Alternatively, you can remember it and then follow it in your mind, or record yourself reading it slowly and play it back.

Before starting make sure that you are warm and comfortable, and try to ensure that you will not be interrupted. Have gentle lighting and burn an oil or incense that helps you to relax. Either sit or lie down, uncross your legs, unfold your arms and close your eyes.

First, focus on your breathing; breathe in through your nose to the count of four, hold the breath for four and then breathe out through your mouth to the count of four. Repeat this several times until you feel truly relaxed.

Imagine you are walking up the side of a gentle hill. You are dressed comfortably and your feet are bare. It has been a hot day which is becoming a beautiful warm evening, and above you the sky is just beginning to darken towards dusk. Beneath your feet the grass is cool and soothing. Ahead you see a forest and as you let your feet lead you towards it you see that it is made up of many different types of tree; there are oak and ash, holly, rowan, yew, beech and elm, and many others. These are the ancient trees of this land, and you can tell that they have been growing here together for a long time. They are well spaced, yet they seem to fit together as though having grown used to one another. A gentle evening breeze stirs their branches lazily. As you approach, you can hear the evening song of the birds. Between the trees you can see a path leading into the wood, and you follow this.

As you step between the trees you feel that the forest seems to welcome you, and the path which you tread is carpeted with moss. The canopy of leaves overhead shuts out the sky, but the remaining light filters through and gives a greenish glow to all around. As you follow the path you hear the sounds of the woodland coming to rest: the scurry of small animals and the creaking of branches.

Now the path you are following slopes gradually away from you, and in the gathering silence you can hear, some way off, the sound of flowing water. Still you walk onwards, along a route which twists in and out between the trees. Sometimes the sound of water seems close, sometimes distant. Although darkness is falling there is enough light for you to see your way, so you continue walking down the gentle slope. The sounds of the life of the night now come to you: the gentle hoot of an owl, the rustle of the leaves and branches as the nocturnal animals start the active part of their day.

Ahead, you see a glimmer of light and the path draws you on towards it. Coming around a group of trees you find yourself on the edge of a broad clearing. Here there is more grass underfoot, and in the centre lies a great expanse of water. The grass slopes gently down to the water's edge, and you walk on until your toes touch the cold, still water. Here there is not a breath of wind and the water's surface is like a great mirror, reflecting the deep blue of the night sky and the silver disc of the full moon above.

You stand for a while, gazing into the reflection; then you become aware of a movement at the other side of the water. As you raise your eyes you see that there are three women standing there. The first is young and clad all in white with flowers in her fair hair; she stands tall and willowy. The second is a woman in her maturity, wearing a dress of red; her long brown hair curls over her shoulders. On her arm she carries a basket of the fruits of summer. The last woman is older, and although stooped and grey-haired, she is nevertheless beautiful. She wears a robe of purple and a cloak of the deepest night sky.

All three women gaze at you across the waters, their eyes seeming to hold all the secrets of the world. As you look at them, one smiles and opens her arms to you. You step forward and instead of your feet walking into the cold waters you find yourself standing directly before her. You hold out your hands and she takes them in hers, and then she speaks to you. The words she says are for you alone, so take a moment to listen to her carefully.

Once she has spoken, she embraces you and you close your eyes. When you open them again, you find that you are back on your own side of the water and the opposite shore is once again empty. You turn and retrace your steps back through the woods. As you go, think about the words that were spoken to you, store them carefully in your mind until their meaning becomes clear.

When you come to the edge of the trees, you find that dawn is breaking and the new day promises to be warm and bright. Now it is time for you to return to your resting self. So close your eyes and focus once again on your breathing. When you are ready, open your eyes, sit upright and rub your arms and legs with your hands.

● ●

George David Fryer

A MEDITATION TO MEET YOUR GUIDE

Visualize a vortex of white energy spinning above your head and then bring this vortex slowly down through your body and out into the earth.

Then, keep recreating vortexes and bringing them through you, each time a little faster until you are in a column of white light.

Once you feel balanced and calm, picture a spotlight in front of you and invite guiding influence' to step into this spotlight.

● ●

Chuck Spezzano

A guided healing meditation I call 'centring' is an excellent way to heal post-traumatic stress, old trauma and conspiracies (traps set up by the ego to make it look like there is no way out). It is one of the few things that heal family patterns and restore bonding.

You simply ask your higher mind (or the Holy Spirit, Christ, Buddha, Quan Yin etc.) to return you to your centre deep within – a place of peace. If you are in a trauma, you simply witness the effect this has on you. Next, you once again ask to be carried to a higher, deeper centre where there is greater peace and innocence. Then, in a while, you ask to be carried to an even higher and deeper centre of peace, innocence and power. After each centring, you witness the effect by how the scene looks and feels. Continue this and bring yourself to utter peace and pure light. This generates the love and joy common to meditation and healing.

Richard Lawrence

As a psychic, one of the most exciting things for me personally has been to receive inspiring messages about the spiritual experiences of those on realms higher than our own physical world. I have not specialized in contacting relatives and friends of the bereaved to bring personal messages of consolation and love. But I have been extremely fortunate to channel a number of poets from different times in history, and I am privileged to share extracts from four of their poems. I've read them at workshops and presentations where they are always well-received.

I used a combination of telepathy and clairaudience (psychic hearing) to channel these. They were received very quickly, almost as fast as I could write them down, but it was not 'automatic writing' – I could have stopped at any time. I am not a poet myself, which may be one reason this style of communication was chosen – to prove its authenticity. It would have simply been impossible for me to construct such poetry in such a short time.

I hope you find these insights from those who have 'been there' as encouraging, hopeful and profound as I do.

A writer who lived some time ago describes immortality as:

> *Now – and now again drink deep the nectar of survival –*
> *Even after time has stopped and wiped from its brow*
> *All man's ills, all humanity's woes,*
> *All the timeless promises of an empty hope that*
> *This thing called life has permanence in mortal currency.*
> *Be gone with such idolatry! For matter means only this –*
> *To live and to experience God in all His forms.*
> *No more than this can mortal existence offer.*
> *But beyond that – reality; beyond that – peace;*
> *And beyond that – well, there in its truest form*
> *Is the dwelling place of Divinity Herself.*

A contemporary songwriter meets his guru in the after-life:

He dealt me a blow,
He banged me to rights,
He told me my faults,
He put up a fight,
He stifled my reason,
He dared me to laugh,
He throttled my anger,
I cried in my heart.
But then he did something
I'll never forget.
He touched me so gently,
My eyes would have wept.
But even that feeling
Was gone with his touch.
My heart was at peace now
He loved me so much.
His hand on my forehead,
His tender eyes beamed,
He looked at my soul now,
I felt it released.

A poet gives her perspective from the 'other side':

When I consider all that passed,
Like worn-out clothing fading fast,
Except one thing, one precious fact –
A very special artefact –
The time I spent in love and peace.
That brings a sense of true release
From foolish thoughts and tired old games,
From rituals with mundane names.

For that is real and that is true.
That will last and then renew
Itself again and yet again.
It grows like flowers in the rain
Until at last they bloom in time
At the height of summer's clime.

A recently deceased DJ discovers his real self in the after-life:

Feel good, deep within a voice said to me
'Be still – don't fight – love is all, it's free.
Give God holy time – all you need to be –
Yourself – In truth – That's all.' We
Will join, as one, all together. He
Told me there and then all there is to see.
I know how it is – how I have to be.
I will share it with whomever comes to me.
That's it – all there is – nothing more – just me
And my inner voice – it has set me free.

● ●

Ian John Shillito

So much history is being forgotten, as each new generation develops its views. Having no history is like having no past; it's like not knowing who your parents were. You wonder, *Where do I belong?*

With the help of spirit, I use my psychic and mediumistic skills to introduce the present to its past. I create a ghost story that overlays a history lesson. Spirit is always up for education and evolution. My ghost investigations are more than just 'scare fests', they are psychic information bureaux.

I believe in knowledge, knowledge of yourself and your surroundings. The world is changing, and we, its inhabitants, are changing too. We have passed through the technological age and are now heading at light speed towards the spiritual age.

As humans, we think we are pretty far down the line of our existence, yet I know we are fairly primitive as a race. Evolution has only just started. It's not over yet!

FUTURE SECRETS

Shelley von Strunckel

Predicting the Future

Being an astrologer is both a gift and a burden. Not only is its complex philosophical tradition endlessly intriguing, it enables me to touch others by offering a unique variety of guidance.

First I was a fascinated student, then a private consultant, working with clients. This involved interpreting their personal horoscopes and the planetary movements to strategize everything from personal decisions to business manoeuvres, the latter benefiting from my background in the commercial world. In 1991 I began writing the daily, weekly and monthly horoscope columns which are now syndicated worldwide. It's hard work, but letters and emails from readers about how my columns have yielded personal insights or been helpful with specific problems more than compensate for the effort.

The downside is the peculiar reaction I sometimes get in social situations. Being an astrologer provokes anything from awe to suspicion. The assumption is that I can predict the future, that I know exactly what's coming, tomorrow, next week, next year or in a decade. And many are convinced that I've got inside information about precisely what's going to happen to them. There have been occasions when I've been introduced to someone who, before I could even say hello, has responded by saying, 'I don't want to know,' and fled!

However, it would be accurate to say that I know more about what's coming than the average individual. Astrology is based on the movement of the heavenly bodies, the sun, moon and planets, through the twelve signs of the zodiac. These have been studied since humanity first settled and began to note the relationship between events in the heavens and those on Earth. These early observations recorded the grand cycles that, on the one hand, make up the great eras of history and that, on the other, astrologers believe shape the more intimate cycles of our daily life.

Today, whether it's an individual reading their horoscope in the newspaper or a client whose personal chart I'm examining, it's not about fortune-telling. It's about transcending the present, seeing a bigger picture. This is no escape from daily life's relentless complexities. Rather, it's an invitation to view life, destiny and free will from an entirely different, more complex and ultimately more practical perspective.

When astrology's principles were first defined, about 4,000 years ago, the world was a metaphysical one, in which life's ups and downs were regarded as being part of a natural, and inevitable, rhythm. Nature dominated, and humanity had no choice but to fit in; the individual had to make the best of their lot. This meant being alert to both the larger cycles and whatever destiny dealt out to them personally. Astrology advised ways to sidestep disasters and take advantage of opportunities – as it has from astrology's dawn until relatively recently.

During the 16th and 17th centuries, the scientific method emerged. This changed the way the world was understood. By focusing only on those realms that can be objectively assessed – weighed and measured – and requiring repeatable experiments, knowledge was literally redefined. The scientific method shaped Western thinking, emphasizing the objective, but at the cost of such unscientific concepts as spirit, soul and various concepts of God and personal emotions. Because these didn't fit, they were sidelined and became second-class studies. The only legitimate prediction was scientific.

While science has done wonders for medicine, space travel and technology, education's focus on objective knowledge has resulted in generations of spiritual illiterates. During this era, students have been taught to revere trained, objective experts but distrust their instincts and personal reactions. Philosophy has become an intellectual exercise rather than a personal journey into life's complexities and, in the case of prediction, the paradox of destiny and free will. Those interested in these subjects had to shift for themselves, attending to their own intuitive and spiritual development, finding teachers by trial and error.

In the scientific model, predictions are expected to be concrete, clear-cut and uncompromising – and if they're correct, they must always be correct. This leaves no leeway for free will. The irony is that the scientific method, which has made it possible to conceive of humanity being liberated from disease and famine, has suppressed the individual spirit.

True, there are times when we'd all like to ignore our responsibilities and abandon ourselves to destiny. Therefore, when under pressure, many turn to predictions of a metaphysical variety – palm reading, cards or horoscopes – hoping they'll eliminate the need to face and deal with challenging situations themselves. Meanwhile others believe that, by ignoring such predictions entirely, they're declaring their free will. Neither is correct.

True, at one point humanity had little choice. Destiny in the form of birth, gender and economic and social conditions determined a fate that only the most courageous and persistent could escape. But things have changed. Grim as today's world sometimes seems, there are growing awareness and increased responsibility – individually, in regard to others and to the planet.

As a result, a new relationship with destiny is being formed. It's no longer fixed, but is negotiable. So, too, prediction must be redefined. It must be viewed as a snapshot of the situation as it stands here and now, reflecting both the circumstances and the attitude of the individual involved, at that time. However, a snapshot captures a passing moment, no more. Change anything – the setting or clothing – and another photo taken, only minutes later, would be completely different.

Similarly, while astrology can very accurately predict the cycles, large and small, with which an individual will be dealing and describe the probable reaction of a star sign or that individual to any particular situation, what the individual actually chooses to do is entirely up to them. They can exercise their free will.

The objective of prediction today, therefore, is not to learn what destiny's dealt out and accept it. Prediction is now about gaining insights about the nature of the times, the likelihood of unexpected twists and surprising turns, and even more importantly, how an individual is likely to react. The task is to assess these, and make a conscious, informed, free-will decision, one that acknowledges predictions as probable developments. This, combined with insights about an individual's nature and the tendencies described by their personal chart or horoscope, gives the advantage of being forewarned – thereby actually increasing free will.

The irony, therefore, is that the individual who seeks out predictions, whatever their nature, could actually be more in charge of their destiny than somebody who avoids them. The person who ignores such prognostications may think that they're free of outside influence. But nobody exists outside the influence of nature's cycles and their own reaction to the issues they're facing.

True power comes not in ignoring the rhythms of the heavens. It comes with respecting their majesty and in observing, understanding and honouring their portents and only once that has been done, making decisions for oneself.

• •

Barefoot Doctor

Q *Secret fantasy to make the world a better place?*

A I get my hands on some secret magic powder, which, though perfectly safe and healthy, when sprayed in the air makes everyone present relax at least 23 degrees more than usual. In that state of relaxation, everyone affected finds themselves being more tolerant and willing to join the global surge towards peace and evolution. Then I spray the whole planet with it.

Q *Future secrets – what do you know about where we're heading?*

A Only a true fool would attempt to answer that but, being quite a fool myself, the scenario I see is an intensification and acceleration of absolutely every thing, both the destructive and the progressive. So, we'll have more and more heavy weather, more floods, droughts and fires, more level to the oceans hence more populated regions submerged, progressively more disease, less food, less drinking water and less oil. On the other hand, we'll have more pooled intelligence and creativity to tackle those problems, hence better husbandry of available resources, better preparations for disasters, better living habits, more sustainable energy and technology, more even distribution of global resources, increased evolutionary rate, hence people performing hitherto unimaginable feats in all areas of life, generally more telepathy and group consciousness and the whole world being run from Beijing.

• •

Robin Lown

Historically speaking, the science of Palmistry has been highly regarded by scholars for thousands of years. Hippocrates and Aristotle knew of and respected it. Rulers like Caesar were also taught it and used it. It is well represented as a psychological tool within many faiths and it is referred to more than once in the Bible.

In the 15 years I've been reading palms, I've found 'balanced hands' predominate. People with these palms have a pragmatic and practical view of life. They represent the group dynamic of needing to have a strong grasp of reality.

It would seem the more scientific, practical and humanitarian aspects of the age of Aquarius are truly upon us. As we move through the next decade, this will filter into

world consciousness, bringing a greater spiritual awareness across the world plus the pressing need to be more
humanitarian in practical ways.

Like a new Renaissance period, fresh, practical and
creative ways of doing things will arrive, through technological innovation, along with the need to help more of
the people, more of the time, across more of our planet.

Sadly, the downside of my research shows that more
people are becoming increasingly toxic. This shows as
shadowy and indistinct hand line formations. It indicates
a worrying slide into developing a confused psyche, a
body less able to fight disease, and greater incidence of
cancers.

The major hand lines are also showing increasing
incidences of emotional losses, meaning that more people
will be touched by loss and affected by disasters than ever
before.

Chuck Spezzano

My most profound, life-changing dream is one where the whole world has leaped into partnership, and we all see each other as friends. I want to help introduce the Age of Friends Helping Friends. So the world recognizes that we are all on the same team, in the same family, on spaceship Earth together. I dream of creating Heaven on Earth with my wife and family and sharing it with the world. I dream that I will live my purpose and embrace my destiny, making the contribution I have come to make and being who I have come to be.

My secret fantasy to make the world better is no secret; I'm busy making it happen: a world of friends helping friends. In my last workshop in China, we focused the mind, heart and spirit of the group to dissolve Hurricane Rita. We also focused on helping those close to us who needed our help using psychological, shamanic and spiritual methods. In my last workshop in Japan, we focused on helping Princess Masako of Japan and, of course, our friends in need. Then during the last two days of the seminar, we also sent love to the earthquake victims in Pakistan, India and Bangladesh. Friends helping friends is not fantasy in my life.

I believe that celestial speed-up will increase for the next seven years, making it possible for us to live in a world of friends helping friends. We have lots of good stuff to do before that happens.

If the world is saved this century, it will be through

business completely remaking itself, and then the world. Many miracles are still needed. Business will take over the job of government by mid-century.

Next century it will be the aboriginal peoples who save the Earth. In this century, they need all of our help and support. Communities of people will learn how to transform themselves and the world around them, making an easy birth for the Earth and its people instead of the traumatic shifts and great loss of life that are predicted.

I believe that Taiwan is the most important country for world peace and transformation in the next fifty years, and that its relationship with China will either be the flashpoint for war and despair, or the bridge that will extend to the rest of the world. It is why I have been spending so much time in Taiwan lately. I want to help make the positive change and build a bridge for the whole world.

The world will leap forward. Now is the time. We're at a crossroads: limp forward or leap forward. If you tell most men that being limp is the alternative to leaping, well, I believe you just motivated them.

Leon Nacson

At some point we are definitely going to stop fighting one another and be forced to concentrate on survival on the planet. We're going to wake up one morning and realize that there's an air problem, a water problem and a soil problem. The only element we didn't pollute is fire. Once there's no point in winning over your neighbour because no one will win as they will die of thirst or hunger, nations will focus on cleaning up their back yard and fixing the planet up so future generations have something to fight over.

• •

David Wells

Q *Deep beliefs that keep you going when things are tough*

A I have faith that everything is for a reason; our earthly heads have to figure out what that reason is and take action. That is the tough part! I absolutely believe in everything I know and that I can cause changes as well as adapt to those that are put upon me by others.

Q *Future secrets – what do you know about where we're heading?*

A We must raise our consciousness as individuals. Do that and everyone around you will want what you have, then their friends will want it and before you know it we will all be more forgiving, more compassionate, and learning, rather than repeating the same old mistakes generation after generation.

Q *Secret fantasy to make the world a better place?*

A Put mums in charge and take all the boys' toys away!

• •

Becky Walsh

One day soon everyone will have the abilities I have. The vibration of the planet is changing. Every dimension vibrates at a frequency to make it solid to us. As our universe changes frequency we will have a stronger connection to the spirit world and maybe even other worlds. You can look around you now and see the change. Part of that change will mean all people reconnecting with their psychic abilities and many people becoming mediums. Animals are not left out of this upgrade, and many will begin to recognize themselves as individuals (my mum's dog already knows itself in a mirror). A few more natural disasters will unfortunately occur but will bring a deeper understanding of ourselves and our world.

Diana Cooper

I have a vision ...

I have a vision of a world at peace, where everyone is well-nourished, educated, spiritually enlightened and happy. It sounds like pie in the sky but I believe it is possible in the lifetime of our children or grandchildren, if enough of us start to adopt some simple principles.

I recognize that my ego is the only thing stopping me from living in abundance, love, joy, health and peace at every moment. And actually your ego is the only thing that stops you from having your heart's desire too. The more I realize this, the easier it is to let go of ego, so that more wonderful energy comes into my life.

Take, for example, envy. In days when I was afraid I was not good enough or successful enough, I thought jealous, envious thoughts about other people who did similar work to myself. That's ego. My energy subtly affected them and, of course, it held me back. Now I bless and encourage everyone's work and help others where I can. My work blossoms and hopefully so does theirs. The fear disappears and I feel peaceful and happy. As far as they allow my thoughts to influence them, the people I bless feel more content too.

Look at hurt. My ego used to hold onto it. Now I ask myself how many lifetimes I am prepared to let myself suffer. And I let go immediately, so that love can come in.

Then, take fear of not having enough, in other words poverty consciousness. Every moment that I am indulging fearful thoughts of lack, whether it is love, money, friends, happiness or success, I am blocking my abundance. Because we are all subtly linked, it blocks yours too. The angels say that poverty consciousness is holding the whole world back.

Opening to abundance consciousness is like switching a light on in your brain. All you do is change your thoughts, words and actions to gratitude and positive expectation. First you thank the Universe for everything good in your life. Then you thank it for everything you are about to receive as if you have already got it and you keep on doing this until, under spiritual law, abundance inevitably flows into your life.

When you know you can draw to yourself whatever you need, all greed or meanness or desire to control disappears like magic. Your heart opens and you can be generous, openhearted, sharing and giving. You are a master and take responsibility for your life. You act with wisdom. Most importantly, you start to respect the planet and every creature on it.

Consciousness is catching. When enough of us decide to embrace abundance consciousness, the leaders of our countries will catch it! And soon this sense of goodwill to those less fortunate will spread. We will find ourselves working in co-operation and harmony throughout the world, honouring each other's race, colour or creed. It is but a step from abundance consciousness to Oneness.

One small thing I do towards accomplishing this takes just two minutes each morning. I light a candle and thank the angels for protecting me, helping me to see the best in others and guiding me to take the highest decisions during the day.

There are two reasons I believe my vision will come about. The first is that the Universe is preparing our planet for 2012, when a rare and extraordinary astrological configuration occurs that happens every 26,000 years. It offers a cosmic moment when things beyond our comprehension can happen. In the past, because of low consciousness on Earth, this configuration led to wars and climate change. This time we are offered the support of the Universe and are riding a great tidal wave towards the light. Angels are flocking to help us. All we have to do is ask; then their assistance is forthcoming to smooth our paths and help us raise our frequencies.

People are unconsciously tuning in to dolphins, the Keepers of Wisdom, who are aligning them to a higher vibration. Unicorns, those pure white creatures of light, are returning to purify us and connect us to our soul energy. Many of the high-frequency energies available in the golden days of Atlantis are being returned to us, the Violet Flame, Reiki, the Mahatma Energy and the higher Rays, amongst others.

Secondly, just as a child is genetically encoded to walk when the time is right, we humans are genetically encoded with extraordinary gifts, talents and spiritual understandings that were fully available to us in Golden Atlantis. At that time we had twelve fully operational strands of DNA. Now we have two that are working. The dormant strands, known as 'junk DNA', are encoded with the sacred gifts we had in Atlantis. As we start to expand our abundance consciousness, our birthright of enlightenment, spiritual connection, psychic gifts and inner peace will be returned to us.

Then the whole world will live in co-operation, harmony, happiness and love. Every person will be educated to develop his or her innate talents so that they can do what they love to do most, and be acknowledged for it. There is enough for all and we will all happily share. The mighty Angels of Atlantis are returning to ensure that this will come about.

In the meantime, give no energy to those who are of lesser understanding. Do not feed with fear or anger the lower conflicts and actions you see around you or in the news. Just bless them. Instead please focus with me on a picture of our planet in divine right order. As we all hold this vision together, at the point of critical mass it must manifest. What a bequest we have it in our power to offer our children and children's children. Let's do it. Thank you.

HOPES & DREAMS

....

Lynne Franks

Understanding the Dream

One of the true gifts of maturity is clarity: being able to distinguish your ego from your essential self and being able to see when you are being pulled out of balance by the needs and illusion of the ego.

We all have dreams of what we want to be or how we see our perfect life. The process of manifesting our dreams is often what gives us hope and keeps us going. But they can become a needless attachment as well. Since I was thirteen I've often let the fantasy of my dreams substitute for the beautiful reality of the moment.

My dreams and visions have ranged from the customary prince coming to rescue me and make me happy, to me actually becoming the warrior princess. And my dream as that warrioress is to make all the ills of the world go away and create a Heaven on Earth based on love and happiness for all.

Time and experience have shown me that all those dreams are ultimately illusion. Whether it's been the perfect romance, the most successful career, the happiest family, youth and beauty or indeed the power to heal the world, I need to look inwards to my own inner peace and self-awareness above and beyond anything.

My spiritual practice has taken me to an acknowledgement of the greater power of the unseen and allowed me to appreciate a new dream, both personal and universal. Having grown up as a post-war baby boomer, I am part of the generation who loved it up in the 60s, then focused on ourselves throughout the remainder of the 20th century, creating a consumer society that has become a threat to the very future of this planet. As someone with a variety of careers in the media, including being a highly successful PR practitioner, and creating SEED as a learning programme for women's sustainable enterprise, I have been at the frontline of these trends with a clear view of our societal patterns and demands.

Unconsciously we have upped the ante by wanting more of everything, and teaching our children to want the same. We wanted the latest technology, the biggest cars, the newest fashions and the most luxurious holidays. In light of all our material desires, perhaps the last and most mature dream we can manifest is to create a global consciousness that will ensure that our grandchildren will have a world to inherit.

On a personal level, my spiritual dreams revolve around the deities, a gathering of gods and goddesses led by the Great Mother herself, who by calling us back to the power of the sacred feminine, reminds us that love, peace and harmony are the keys to happiness, not the biggest house on the block or the most money in the bank.

Now a grandmother in my fifties, I have found my true self accompanied by beings on all planes who have nurtured and taught me. By practising Raja Yoga meditation with the female-led Brahma Kumaris, by experiencing Shamanic rituals in the Ecuadorian jungle with the indigenous Achuar Nation, from embracing the power of initiation with the Spirit Horse tribe in their beautiful rugged home in Pennant Valley, Wales, and dancing the Five Rhythms on mountain tops with Gabrielle Roth and her merry band of tantric warriors, I have caught glimpses of a new way of being.

I have seen a way forward where, by respecting and loving each other and the planet which is our home, we can create communities that can learn from each other through our storytelling, through our poetry and through our dance. I've seen that by taking the best of the technology and science of the modern world and combining these with the wisdom and rituals of ancient times, and by honouring Mother Earth in all things, we can consciously create a new future of infinitesimal possibilities that offers hope to all those who are coming after us.

Dawn Breslin

My secret fantasy to make the world a better place would be to have creativity centres for maximizing human potential – places where unemployed, homeless and socially excluded groups, dyslexics, and any person who has been given a label that says that this is the end of their potential, can learn to play and realize the power they have, together with on-tap guidance from people who would truly nurture and care for them.

· ·

Alla Svriniskaya

My deep passionate dream for a brighter future is that our children learn about energy awareness – the energy of their bodies and the environment – early in their lives. It is a priceless time to teach people how to 'travel inside yourself', how to reflect and understand your feelings. Children are also fantastic at learning meditations, as they are great with fantasies.

We protect children so much, they don't know how to deal with the negative energy exchange in adult life and learning can become very painful without the appropriate tools. At school they must learn about breathing techniques, the power of intention, how to recharge etc. When we give our children tools to connect with their soul, aura and energy, they will find it much much easier to build up their own unique core and boundaries.

We are also teaching our kids too much about control – 'Don't do this, don't do that …' We are not teaching self-expression. We can't fully understand life and find our true place in it just using our intellect. Intuition is our inner voice to lead us to our unique path. We must develop and learn how to trust and follow our intuition from the earliest stages of our lives.

I believe that our soul is given to us with our life for evolution. We are responsible for it to be cleaner and fuller at the time of our death than at birth. Soul turns our mind into conciousness, which is what's needed in our world today to free us from our fears and unite us.

• •

Joan Hanger

I have a fantasy to get all the most powerful people in the world together in one room and make them understand that something has to done to correct the poor conditions of the world's children.

My most profound dream came when I'd approached Kensington Palace to have an interview with the late Princess of Wales. Prior to receiving a reply from the Palace, I dreamt of two babies, both wrapped in bunny-covered blankets, and one kept rolling out and chatting to me madly! I kept putting the bunny blanket back and rolling the baby up tightly but then it would unwind and start chatting again and again. I awoke knowing that I would be successful in my attempt to interview the Princess because the babies were so dominant. Babies in dreams often depict new beginnings and new happenings in our lives. The experience of becoming a friend of the Princess was life-changing in so many different ways.

It's natural that sensual and sexual dreams entertain our nocturnal adventures because sex is part of our society and way of life.

My most spooky dream was when I had been diagnosed with breast cancer at the age of 50. The night before my operation to remove my right breast, I dreamt in clear black and white of an obituary column. As I frantically checked down this column for my name or any of my children's names, I felt huge relief that none of our names was there. More at ease, I went off to have my operation and thankfully it was a successful one.

• •

Gordon Smith

My friend Dronma is a Tibetan Buddhist who does a lot of prayers and healing for people. When I want prayers done for someone, to send them on to the other side, I ask Dronma to help.

My English springer spaniel Charlie, whom I had for ten years, had to be put to sleep last year after he contracted an incurable, human form of leukemia that had never been heard of in dogs. Now, Dronma had quite a connection to Charlie; she always thought his consciousness was human and even drew him at a spiritual circle, saying he'd be coming to me, before I got him. So she kindly did a Tibetan Buddhist practice for him, to send him over to the other side. She would have worked through the *Tibetan Book of the Dead*.

On the sixth night going into the seventh day, just as I was coming to consciousness, in an almost waking dream, I had a lovely experience. I heard Charlie bark in a place where I used to play as a child.

I went to walk towards Charlie but felt a force stop me and a man's voice saying, 'No, you can't go get him yet, because you'll pull him back. This is an important stage for him.'

I went to take a step forward and this buzzing wall of golden bees appeared. They weren't harming me, but I couldn't walk through them, so I turned back.

The man said, 'Just go, he's fine. Listen to him!' I could hear how happy he was, barking away. I woke up with a nice thought about him being somewhere where he was being looked after and helped.

A couple of days later, I called Dronma to tell her about my strange dream. She said, 'I put a wall of bees up to protect Charlie from you. I knew you wouldn't walk through a wall of bees. I've been wearing a bee necklace for these first crucial seven days of his progressing, when a consciousness can be held back by sympathy. I just took it off this morning when I woke. That tells me that he's gone on a level and can't be pulled back. For his consciousness to expand and grow on the other side, he needs to be free of his physical memories for the first seven days. Charlie is now free to move on.'

Wow! I felt such huge relief. And it really brought home to me the power of prayer.

• •

Leon Nacson

My most profound, life-changing dream was when my dearly departed father appeared in a dream, put his arms around me and said, 'Come on son, leave this. It's time for a relaxing beer.'

At the time I was so possessed by my publishing schedule, the upcoming events and tours and my media commitments. What I was doing was defining me and my life was one deadline after another.

I have always been able to solve any challenges during my dreams. By sleeping on a problem, the answer to what I really want to do is there in my dreams to decode upon waking.

Carina Coen

I have had many unusual dreams but the most recent, life-changing one happened when my beautiful mermaid-and-dolphin handpainted picture, on the wall above my head in the bedroom of my apartment, came to life one night. It was as though the top half of the room became water. The mermaid floated above me singing and talking with immense passsion, and the dolphin beamed with happiness.

According to this mermaid, part of my mission is to return others to their inner souls. She reminded me of the need for self-communication and the coming of affinity in 2008.

The mermaid said that this was the time of a huge wake-up call to WATER SOS – Save Our Souls and Save Our Seas! She urged me to make my Mercarina holistic wellbeing work more of a reality in the world. She advised to make my bedroom an office of communication between the oceans and the forests (lungs) of the world for purification. The very next day I moved my bed to my mezzanine and purchased an 8-shaped red desk as the centrepiece to the office. She certainly made me move! And it's worked.

I now work with Marine Connection (www.marineconnection.org) and Save The Amazon Rainforest Organization (www.staro.org). Mercarina is a wonderful work-in-progress, incorporating the arts, holistic health, beauty and healing, plus insights into life and how we can change and save our lives while we still have a chance.

••

David Wells

I once dreamt I was at a party with many faces I seemed to recognize; one of them I felt was a well-known Spiritual being. He was standing at the opposite end of the room to me. He removed the hood of his robe so that I could see him. I smiled and he smiled back, then I woke up.

Days later, at my astrology class, my teacher said to me that his Ascended Master had asked that next time I see him at a party, could I at least say hello! I had not discussed my 'dream' with anyone. It changed my outlook on where exactly we go when we sleep …

••

Chris Fleming

Waking dreams

My most profound, life-changing dream was of my sister drowning and me standing there watching her drown. A white life preserver passed by my eyes and missed my sister. When I woke I told my mom, and she said to run and get help if that ever happened.

Six months later, my two-year-old sister fell into a pool with no parents around. I ran and got help while all the other kids stood there frozen to the spot. I recognized it was just like the dream I'd had. I saved my sister. My parents pulled her out just as she went under. She had a snowsuit on that filled up with water and then sunk just as they reached for her. A few seconds more and it would have been too late. I was only four or five years old.

But I remember long before that even. My first memory is of watching my mom and dad at the park film a squirrel and my mom's tummy being swelled. I wasn't born yet.

Divine sleep

I have had a few divine-intervention situations that I look back on and always know that I'm looked after. Once, I was driving home when I started to fall asleep and almost went into oncoming traffic. I banged the steering wheel with my fists and asked God to protect me and not let me fall asleep as I had crashed a car a year before by dozing off at the wheel.

Moments later my head went backwards as I fell asleep. As this happened, I felt someone whack my nose, like a finger snapping at an ear lobe. I pulled my head up to see myself now in the oncoming lane with cars coming right for me. I swerved out of the way back into my lane as I heard their horns blaring in the background. I was shocked and imagined an explosion and me going through the windshield.

I soon realized that if my nose had not been flicked I wouldn't have woken up and avoided the disaster. I looked to the passenger seat and smiled as my nose still stung. Someone or something there had saved my life.

Wake-up call

I hope one day the world will wake up and realize that as we continue to separate ourselves, we are destroying ourselves. We need to be united as a world no matter what our beliefs, colours or status. If we don't we will always have war, we will always be in trouble. We must stop the separation and start the peace and unity. Fear is causing us to separate and has become the biggest evil. And too many are using it to their advantage. The Earth will continue to change to force us to unite, but instead of uniting we may do the opposite. Every day I see negativity, separation and lies. When will it end? Or is it just the beginning? The spirits are calling out to us with warnings, but is anyone listening? I hope so.

Sarah Dening

Hidden Knowledge

When I was about 21, I had a strange dream. I was in Ancient Egypt, inside a pyramid. About two-thirds of the way up one of the walls was a shaft, at the foot of which was a wide ledge on which I lay down. I looked up into the shaft, which slanted upwards through the pyramid to the night sky above. Shining directly down on me was a bright star or planet. It seemed that I came regularly to this place to receive energy from the star, rather like recharging a battery. I knew that eventually, when my time on Earth was over, I would lie down on this ledge so that my soul could return home to the star.

At that time, I knew almost nothing about Ancient Egypt. Years later, however, I was astonished to find a book about the King's Chamber in the pyramid of Cheops at Giza. People had assumed its slanting shafts were just for ventilation. But this book proposed that they were focused on the constellation of Orion, to enable the soul of the deceased to return 'home'. Could this explain my dream? Had I somehow made contact with a previous incarnation, perhaps, or an obscure racial memory? Can we, in fact, access hidden knowledge through our dreams? Experience has shown me we can.

I have always been interested in the big questions of life: Who are we? What is the purpose of our life? I studied metaphysics, practised meditation and explored

Christianity but it was not until I discovered the work of Carl Gustav Jung that the final pieces of the jigsaw fell into place. His views on the importance of dreams, the relationship between the masculine and feminine sides of the psyche and the nature of synchronicity made sense. I longed to know more and entered analysis.

Quite early on in this process, I had a dream that determined the direction my life would take. In it, I was in a college, hanging around outside a room in which Professor Jung was giving a lecture to some advanced students. Suddenly the door opened, and there stood Jung himself. He invited me to join the class. When I woke up, I knew that I would become a therapist myself. And so it has been.

In recent years, readers of my weekly national newspaper columns have sent me their dreams for interpretation. A significant proportion of these feature death. Since death in dreams symbolizes transformation, it seems that many people are subconsciously yearning for a profound change of perspective. I think that this must involve a rebalancing of the two fundamental sides of our nature, our masculine and feminine, or yin and yang, energies. How? One way, based on hidden knowledge dating back to the Ancient Egyptian mysteries, is revealed in a book I am currently co-writing with a healer. My secret fantasy is that it will help to bring about the shift of consciousness we so clearly want and need.

....

Barefoot Doctor

Q *Who or what inspires you most, and why?*

A What – Witnessing displays of human courage against all odds, whether it's someone overcoming a dreaded disease, or battling out of a job they hate, taking a crazy chance on living their life's dream and achieving it. Witnessing displays of human compassion, especially on a mass scale, say in the wake of a tragedy such as the Asian tsunami or the London bombings.

Who – The counter-culture hero and maverick psychiatrist R.D. Laing, with whom I had the privilege of studying and unravelling the complexities of my own psyche back in the late '70s. Him, John Lennon (who without doubt was an avatar in human form), Jesus (or at least the myth I have of him, in respect of being a healer) and Chuang Tsu, the bumbling genius superhuman ancient Chinese Taoist master of yore, for his supreme clarity and undeniable sense of humour in the face of a ridiculous world (even back then).

Q *Deep beliefs that keep you going when things are tough?*

A That everything moves according to the immutable law of yin and yang, dark and light, easy and difficult, and that one inevitably transforms into its opposite and back and so on *ad infinitum*. Thus, tough changes to easy and vice versa, so there's no need to get too hung up on any particular phase of the cycle, neither gloating with the good, nor becoming defeated by the bad. I'll repeat, *'Out of this darkness will come great light,'* and that usually gets me through the worst bits.

● ●

Judi James

Despite being someone who advertizes the need for goal-setting, I am still very inspired and motivated by negative emotions like anger. If you want to see me achieve, just tell me I can't do something! For some reason the idea of proving people wrong and spitting in their eye (metaphorically speaking) can get me really fired up.

I was therefore most inspired by a teacher at my grammar school who terrified me and insisted I was no good at English. I put in a lot of hard work trying to prove the old bag wrong and I always credit my six novels and eight non-fiction books to her!

I went to a school reunion with the specific idea of telling her but, although she seemed to have shrunk, she still scared the pants off me so I said nothing.

I like to keep inspiring myself so I'm always having a go at myself and telling myself off. It seems to do the trick!

Michele Knight

I've always wanted to encourage people to embrace their own power and be the magician of their lives. So I give readings which offer transformation rather than a reliance on fate.

Life is comprised of a series of moments; some good, some bad, some tragic or triumphant, and none of these can be held or saved. Each moment passes, the best and the worst, flowing in and out like an unpredictable ocean. It's essential to see the bigger picture and not get caught up in the minutiae of life.

When things are incredible or desperate we can stand transfixed in the moment believing that it will always be like this. We believe we will always be this joyous or depressed. Look back now to three, five, ten years ago. Do you recognize yourself? Do you have the same views, emotions, loves?

If we could raise ourselves above these moments and view our lives as a whole, things would be very different. Seeing this moment as eternal is like entering quicksand, it sucks you under into an illusion. If the moment is fantastic, surf it like a wave, be in it, but be aware that it shall pass. The enigma is that all we really have is this moment. To accept and to be in the moment is pure magic.

In the moment you can make changes which rumble through the whole of your life and transform its direction. Having faith in the moment, however hideous or glorious, is an opportunity for a personal revolution.

Life is a bigger picture; the worst betrayals I have experienced were a gateway to the joy of my life now. They had incredibly painful consequences at the time, but led to major miracles. Losses can destroy your old life and lead to a life beyond your expectations.

Many years ago, a partner left me for an old friend. I was devastated. I was so caught up in commitment, I had no idea how destructive the relationship had become or how far I had strayed from my path. Sometimes we refuse to see the reality of our lives, so the Universe gives us a blessing disguised as a big kick.

This led to me transforming my whole life from the roots up, leaving London and living the life I had always dreamed of, with horses, donkeys and a thatched cottage in the country. I also experienced a new deeper relationship than I ever thought possible and still thank my old friend in my prayers for the gift of releasing me from an outworn life.

Sometimes we avoid following our heart or our dreams because of what others will think. We stay in situations because we feel it is the right thing to do or the other person won't cope without us. But this is disrespectful to the sacred in others. The magic of change is available to all of us and we all have the power to tap into it.

This life is just a flap of a butterfly's wing in time. So gather your soul up and ask yourself what you want to overcome and achieve. You are worthy of many miracles. You are worthy of happiness, forgiveness, abundance and love. Never give up!

• •

Pauline Kennedy

My first awareness of my healing abilities came at a Stuart Wilde lecture in the mid-1980s. During a break a woman sitting near me got a migraine. I laid my hands on her forehead and neck and visualized the pain dispersing. She said she felt a fire shooting though my hands into her head and within a few minutes the migraine had gone. That was a turning point for me and was the beginning of a practical 'hands-on' journey into the healing arts.

My most treasured possession is my sense of humour which has pulled me through some very dark moments and also enables me to connect with and lift other people's spirits too. Laughter and joy are powerful healers.

My spirit guides have been with me since I was small. They nearly all take the forms of animals. I don't talk about them as I hold that in doing so you dissipate their power. I always feel protected and am guided incredibly well by them all. They always help out when I ask. You must ask for direction from your guides otherwise they remain impartial observers.

My deep beliefs act as my anchors. They are:

Live for the moment,
Work on, trust and listen to your inner self,
Forgive yourself and others – always,
Respect everything as everything has its place, even the bad,
Be, don't do,
Detach, don't judge,
If you don't like something change yourself,
Protect and nurture all creatures and growing things that don't speak human (that includes Aliens),
Stay awake, aware, alive (look both ways when crossing the road),
And be honest,
Be loving even when it hurts,
Honour and do your bit for the environment,
Give back at least ten times more than you take,
Eventually, if you keep focused, set intent and declutter your baggage, life will shift gear for the better,
Be patient, wise, kind, loving,
Seek joy and trust in the magic of life.

We are in the process of a huge planetary awareness shift. I believe there's a huge battle going on between good and evil like never before in the deeper psychological levels of mankind's psyche. We are in a make-or-break period but also one of great positive transformation and possibilities. It's an amazing time where we have the chance to truly understand our existence here, to fully realize our potential and start focusing on our magnificent role as caretakers and creators, not destroyers and despots.

• •

Hazel Courteney

How would you feel about the way you view your world if you knew with absolute certainty that life after death and reincarnation are a fact? Also, that all of us are capable of miracles and that our thoughts help create every aspect of our physical world?

Well, having undergone an incredible near-death experience in 1998 with a medical doctor present, which triggered huge amounts of paranormal phenomena around me, I now see the world though different eyes.

Following my near-death, I began seeing everything, including us, as beings of energy or frequency, and could clearly hear and see other dimensions. My energy field began crashing electronic equipment, I developed the ability to change TV channels just by looking at the screen, became super-psychic and much more.

As a journalist I was determined to find rational explanations for what happened to me, and during the intervening years, I have met many others who have also undergone intense spiritual awakenings, plus several world-renowned scientists who have shared their research, which felt right to the depths of my soul.

There is now such a huge body of evidence from people such as Gary Schwartz, professor of psychology at the University of Arizona, Professor David Fontana at the University of Liverpool, and several other research institutes – demonstrating that consciousness definitely survives physical death, that it's now up to the sceptics to prove that it doesn't.

There is also a wealth of science on how reincarnation, telepathy and many miracles are possible, from scientists such as Emeritus Professor Bill Tiller (www.tiller.org) at Stanford University in the USA.

All that I learned from these scientists resonated with what I had intuitively known during my experience. For instance, what we tend to think of as being solid, physical matter, is little more than *organized* energy – and the single most important factor that organizes energy into matter *is our sustained intentions.*

Most importantly I was able to see many of our possible futures. I now know that we all have far more choice as to what happens in our futures than most people realize. Yes, certain major events have been 'set in stone' for thousands of years – or at least set in motion by events millennia ago – but the rest of what happens depends on our thoughts and actions on every level.

For instance, on a physical level, if you live on burgers, chips and junk food, then you are creating a potential future of diabetes, heart disease and stroke. Or you can choose to eat more healthily, in which case you have the potential for a healthier future.

Everything is frequency – your foods and your thoughts emit specific frequencies. Frequencies carry huge amounts of information. Every cell in your body emits its own unique range of frequencies (information) which are as unique to you as your DNA. And people who know this are able to 'hear' and interpret these frequencies, hence psychics can know so much about you without ever having met you.

Scientists have also shown that if sufficient people – one in every 100 – can send out consistent, concentrated, positive, loving thoughts (frequencies) to their loved ones and our world, then the *accumulation* of loving thoughts begins to create an invisible lattice grid all around us – which can eventually manifest into our physical world. Our thoughts can literally help to stop wars, reduce violence and stress – and they can heal people.

This has been proven and verified in numerous, independent scientific experiments around the world. Log on to the Global Consciousness Project, based at Princeton Uinversity, US, on http://noosphere.princeton.edu/ or the Maharishi University site on www.mou.org and www.mum.edu.

The biggest soul secret is to begin to realize just how special *your* contribution can be to this world. Begin today by eating more healthy foods, then start thinking more positively – this alone will boost your immune system. Work on developing an inner knowing that everything will work out fine – and smile more. Your happiness will affect others and you start a chain reaction. Next, do what you can, when and where you can, to help others and the planet. Keep repeating to yourself over and over every day, 'Everything is perfect.'

In these ways way you will increase your spiritual growth and help humanity to take the next 'giant leap forward'.

● ●

Alberto Villoldo

Shamans don't rely on beliefs, they rely on experience. Belief is the stuff of religion, whereas experience is the stuff of spirituality. That's the difference between religion and spirituality, that one of them is based on experiences that happened to someone 2000 years ago, and the other is based on the experiences that you're having right now.

When things are bad for me, I pray. I ask for blessings from Heaven and Earth and my suffering lifts. We differentiate between suffering and pain. Pain is an inevitable part of life, but suffering is avoidable. It's what happens in your mind, to make you out as a victim.

William Bloom

Q *Astro details*

A Sun and moon are in Aquarius. Cancer rising.

Q *First memory*

A Playing with my mum.

Q *Deep beliefs that keep you going when things are tough*

A When things are tough, I tend not to struggle or complain. It's a waste of energy to fight the cycles of life. There's a useful piece of Buddhist advice – *What matters is not your suffering. What matters is your attitude towards your pain.*

Q *Who or what inspires you most and why?*

A I am inspired most by parents I know who care for special-needs children. Some of these children are adolescents and adults. Whatever the circumstances and the available support, the emotional exhaustion, suffering and self-sacrifice are enormous. And beneath it all is this enduring and mysterious love.

It reminds me to focus on core ethics of unconditional love and not be distracted by feel-good selfishness. I'm reminded of the soul's drive to heal and redeem, and to be humble and congruent.

Q *Secret fantasy to make the world a better place*

A I believe it is possible to create Heaven on Earth, for all peoples to live in harmony with each other and with nature. My biggest dream is to see every house on the planet powered by 100% clean energy and a village green with fountains, clean water and a children's play area every 100 yards in every city.

Q *Future secrets – what do you know about where we're heading?*

A I believe that grace and miracles are happening all the time. Equally, I believe we must be realistic that the great tides of history and humanity's collective karma may take millennia to unfold into harmony.

The secret is to be naively hopeful and wisely realistic. Then we need to work with great courage and endurance to build utopia even if we do not see it in our own lifetimes.

Paradise for everyone is inevitable, but we have to work for it.

Stuart Wilde

The Feminine Strength of Surrender

It is easy to become indignant at the evil of the world, and the way the planet and its animals are mistreated. It is all very sad. Yet your soul can become wet wading through rivers of injustice that you are powerless to fix. Sometimes the weight of helplessness and futility hangs over us like a shroud. We lose touch with beauty as we become blinded by a silent rage. You can soon lose sight of your true self and which way to go.

Some years ago, I mounted my high horse of indignation and I went out to fight evil. I scored some fantastic successes but I suffered more defeats. In the end I got tired and sick, and nearly died a few times along the way.

Eventually, I realized fighting evil is stupid. I took to an idea I call 'cheesy denial'. You smile and pretend every-thing is just fine. But cheesy denial becomes painful because it endorses a lot of lies. So, as a cure for cheesy denial, I tried isolation for three-and-a-half years, but I got lonely. So now I'm twiddling my thumbs waiting for a new formula. I think it's called surrender.

I've reconciled it in my heart by realising two important things: powerlessness is a part of people's karma in this life; we have to be gracious and accept it. And, while injustice is a terrible thing, we can see an improvement in the world over recent decades as humanity becomes more and more conscious and aware of itself. Also, in being aware of injustice and watching it, we learn what it is that we don't what to become.

Beauty lies in surrender. It's a feminine humility that calls to our wounded souls from beyond the ancient mists of Avalon. Late at night I'd call to the ladies of the mist saying, 'Help me, my heart, she cry.' And sometimes the Spirit of Surrender would whisper to me in visions and dreams, and she would tell me to quit and sit and wait. So to while away the time I'd breathe love into the hearts of liars and crooks and paedophiles and the embezzlers of human souls, and I felt better as I waited as instructed.

Most of the evil is masculine yang, and all of the glorious histories of which society is so proud are simply gruesome accounts of pillage, mass murder and conquest. Humanity is but a child sick with a terrible imbalance of yang that has lasted several thousand years. It's an evolutionary phase like the antics of a rebellious teenager. There is no point in fighting it, for in the emotion of your antagonism you abandon the very softness that offers you reconciliation and redemption.

We are all changing and growing. And in the collective nightmare of our humanity, a golden light trickles through in the dead of night liberating people as fast as they will embrace a new ideal. We have to be grateful for small mercies, there are many people on the spiritual path who are trying to escape and take others with them. Understanding that, we should be patient and surrender, for there is gentleness in that. And anyway, over a long enough time-frame the masculine yang will burn itself out and the feminine yin will triumph.

To go with the softness, it's best not to get too hung up with people's deficiencies but rather look to their heroic redeeming qualities, while of course fixing yourself, all the while. To change who you are, it's good to learn to meditate so you can lower your brain oscillations away from waking ideas more into subtle feelings and alternative realities.

This soft but strong femininity is a very great power that we know little about. But it has shown that it will sustain you once you start to break free, and it graciously holds you up when you begin to doubt or feel a bit wobbly. Know that you are not alone.

The trick is not to confront the system while you are trying to leave it. I was a bit too brash in this life; I should have kept my mouth shut. There is a stupidity in confronting the system, because that which you confront holds you invisibly by the wrist, not allowing you to get away.

But I learned my lessons and eventually I retreated. Once I put down the cudgel of my indignation and I embraced the feminine spirit, the humility of her world gradually built a bridge for me and I saw the way out. Respite is there for every weary soul to be blessed with a second chance as they all should be.

Laura Berridge

We stand at a time in history when the feminine energy, which has been suppressed and judged for thousands of years, is rising up again to bring us and the world we live in back into balance. My work frees women up to value their femininity – to recognize their inner gifts and life purpose and bring their unique beauty physically, emotionally and spiritually to their world.

As we reclaim our full potential as women we will remember that we are all Divine and connected in Oneness and love. I know that the miracle healing stories I have experienced have prepared me to be a teacher of this. My journey has taken me through working with many archetypal energies and facets of the deities: Artemis, Venus, Kali, Magdalene and Isis. Yet I have also worked through their collective shadow side and their legacy of grief and loss.

Now I'm working with Lakshmi, who is celebrated in India as divine consort of God Vishnu, bringer of good fortune, light, love and beauty. We've all had enough hardship and I feel Lakshmi represents the abundance and wholesome wellbeing of divine partnership, enlightenment and sharing Heaven on Earth.

Cassandra Eason

Some of my most helpful beliefs:

- Today is the tomorrow I worried about yesterday, so if the bad thing doesn't happen, or even if it does, I wasted yesterday fretting about what I couldn't change anyway.

- If you do something kind for others when you can, then when you are tired or really down someone will show kindness to you – a sort of cosmic piggy bank.

- Say something nice to someone who is being rude, patronising or bloody-minded and you suddenly get the power back in the situation.

- Life basically is good and if we think the best of people then usually they will justify that faith in the end. This has helped me to believe all my children would find the right path if I gave them space and approval.

- There is no right time, no perfect moment, so if I want to do something I launch it with a kick-start and hope the energies catch up.

- Most importantly I believe the things we regret most are the ones we never tried and so I do generally say yes to most things however unpromising, and even when it has been a disaster I am glad I had the experience.

Some inspirational predictions:

- Within thirty years a race or tribe of people will be discovered who have preserved their culture fairly intact. They will inspire popular consciousness to aim for an older, slower way of life (even for those in the fast lane) and will have a far-reaching impact.

- After an explosion of hyperactivity and attention-deficit disorders among the young and the new adult generation, within ten years there will be a complete turnaround against computer games, mobile phones and violent films in the general population and an attraction for the simpler, gentle approach to life.

- Alternative healing will become part of mainstream medicine in the next twenty years, as a result of even more dramatic discoveries of the toxicity of modern medicines. There will be a return to considerations about the quality of life rather than prolonging physical years for the sake of it.

Wyatt Webb

I am privileged to participate in a process where people heal a lifetime of wounds that have interfered with them experiencing their birthright of emotional and spiritual freedom – a condition known as 'the joy of living'.

I don't have a secret fantasy to make the world a better place, rather an open, loudmouthed belief that as a world culture we desperately need to grow up and take responsibility for our thoughts, feelings and behaviours. Once and for all, we must all conquer our fear and self-loathing so that we might stop attacking and blaming, and start nourishing, sharing our cultures openly and allowing each other the freedom to be authentic.

SECTION TWO –

WELLBEING;
HEALTH AND HEALING;
DIET AND EXERCISE;
BEAUTY

Doreen Virtue

Q *Sun sign and other planetary influences*

A Sun: Taurus
Moon: Virgo
Rising: Capricorn
Venus: Pisces
Mars: Pisces

I'm so grateful that I'm a triple-earth sign, as this helps me to stay grounded whilst teaching very esoteric information.

Q *First memory*

A Peering over the crib to see my baby brother, Kenny. I was one-and-a-half when he was born.

Q *Most treasured possession and why?*

A While I deeply appreciate and greatly enjoy all that I have, I don't feel attached to any of it.

Q *Top tip for meditation*

A I feel like I'm in a constant state of meditation, and in a trance so much that I rarely drive a car (except very short distances, like to the market down the street). I've set up my life so that I don't have to go into my left brain very often. I have attracted wonderful friends, family members and employees who do the left-brain stuff that I need wonderfully well.

Q *Secret way of pampering or healing yourself that makes you feel amazing*

A I have two main hobbies that are pure fun and I always do once a week – scuba diving and belly dancing. I take classes on both continuously, and find they remove me from earthly concerns and take me to a bliss that's unlike anything else I've experienced.

I love scuba diving because it allows me to be totally free, to 'fly' underwater without having to come back up to the surface for air. It's completely quiet underwater. You don't hear telephones, cars or airplanes. Just the sound of your breath. I love communing with the undersea life, including the fish, turtles, dolphins, manatees, and my other friends of the sea. My memories of Atlantis are heightened when I'm scuba diving.

Belly dancing is a wonderful way to exercise, connect with the goddess, and to clear the chakras. It's one of the most ancient forms of dance and a beautiful expression of divine feminine grace and power. I love dancing with scarves, as a form of colour therapy. I was divinely guided to take belly-dance lessons. I felt right at home from my first class, and I've met some wonderful female friends there.

Q *Diet or exercise tip which really works*

A I believe we all receive divine guidance about our diet and exercise programs which work best for ourselves. There's no one right way for everyone. I strongly suggest following whatever guidance you're receiving, and make those positive changes in your diet and lifestyle according to your intuitive nudges.

For me personally, a chemical-free organic vegan diet and daily cardiovascular exercise work best. I've exercised daily for twenty years, and have been a vegan (animal-free diet) since 1996. This combination keeps my energy really high, so I don't need caffeine or other drugs. I definitely received help from the angels when I was detoxing and letting go of some of my food addictions. The angels help us all with these issues, if we'll just ask.

Q *Secret lucky charm / ritual / mantra for good luck*

A I don't believe in 'luck' in the sense that good fortune occurs in happenstance ways. I definitely believe in, and practise, the power of prayer, affirmations and visualisation.

My parents taught me how to channel the power of positive thoughts, intentions and feelings when I was little. Dad had quit his aerospace-engineer job to pursue the career of his dreams (building and writing about model aeroplanes). We used prayer, affirmations and visualization to put food on the table, pay our bills and get a new family car. My parents are still in excellent health and my father's just now starting to turn grey (he's in his 80s). I credit this to the fact that they live their dreams and don't compromise.

They passed this legacy onto me, and I feel very fortunate to have such amazing parents.

Q *Deep beliefs that keep you going when things are tough*

A Don't focus upon the illusion of problems – affirm that there's underlying peace, resolution and order. The more you focus upon solutions instead of problems, the more peace and wonderful results you attract to yourself.

Q *Secret fantasy to make the world a better place*

A Everyone realising that this is an abundant universe, and there's no need for struggle or competition. There's plenty for everyone to spare and share.

Q *Most loving thing you've done recently but haven't told anyone*

A If I told you, I'd violate my self-pact about doing secret giving and helping. Let's just say that I give a lot. I am internally divinely guided to donate a lot of money and time. I am told by the angels which organisations and people to give donations and other forms of support to.

Q *If you could be a deity who would you be and why?*

A One reason why I love the goddesses and male ascended masters is because they represent aspects of all of us, as well as aspects of the Creator. So it's easy to see parts of yourself in the various gods and goddesses. I work closely with Kali, Lakshmi, Quan

Yin, Mary, Ganesha and other deities, depending on the situation I'm in. So to choose one would be impossible.

Q *Future secrets – what do you know about where we're heading?*

A I've seen the same vision for a long time: the future is wonderful!! We're returning to Eden, by way of the new Indigo, Crystal and Rainbow children who are here as role models, pushing out the old energy of competition, lack-mentality and dishonesty while ushering in the new energy of co-operation, manifestation and integrity.

In the future, we'll all manifest our needs, either with our inborn spiritual alchemical abilities, or by working in a trade aligned with our deepest passions and true interests. We'll get away from eating processed or cruelty-based foods, and eat natural diets based upon compassion for animals and plants. The angels show me that global warming will lead to worldwide tropical atmospheres with lots of lush plants and tropical fruits. This will provide fresh air. The melting polar ice caps will provide fresh water. It's all in divine order. We needn't fear the changes which are occurring. They're all good in the end.

WELLBEING SECRETS

Stephen Langley

My interest lies in understanding and treating the body, mind and spirit. I have spent some 20 years of study which has culminated in degrees and diplomas in naturopathic medicine, herbal medicine, colon hydrotherapy, homoeopathy, Chinese medicine and transpersonal psychology.

It has taken me to various places in the world where I have studied the healing methods of many different cultures. I've worked with the Kahunas (Spiritual healers of Kauai in the Hawaiian Islands), Lamas in Tibet and Zen monks in Japan, to name but a few.

I have also spent time with the very old and healthy people of Kashmir; part of the Himalayas where people live the longest on this planet. I learnt a lot about the food they ate and the water they drank. The key is not so much 'what we eat or drink' but 'what we absorb'. As we age we need to look at how we can maximize absorption – both in the type of food that we take in and the water we take for granted.

If things ever get tough, I put myself into a very relaxed state and meditate. I try and return to my true centre and the right answer or direction will always come. I use a

Zen form of meditation which is quick and straight to the point. I learnt how to do this whilst living in a Zen monastery in Kyoto, Japan. It works through rhythmic breathing coupled with emptying the mind by focusing on a point about one metre in front of the eyes.

I am happiest when I reconnect with nature. I love walking barefoot on the grass wherever I am in the world, listening to the Earth's heartbeat.

I am inspired by all things that help raise our consciousness. I believe we are all here to learn and grow and that we are all responsible for whatever happens to us through our own consciousness.

My greatest interest is in transcendent experience or spiritual awakenings. My studies in transpersonal psychology enabled me to interview and document a number of people who believed that their spiritual 'shift' or 'change in consciousness' enabled them to go into full remission from their cancers. This was further proof to me that we are spiritual beings living in a material world and the world is essentially homoeopathic – we get what we are, not what we think we want.

The Spiritual will alter or affect the way we think (Mind).

The way we think will alter or affect the way we feel (Emotions).

And the way we feel will alter or affect our bodies (Physical).

In essence all illness is at some level a manifestation of the human mind. The body will conform to the Spiritual.

To put it succinctly, the state of our health is:

- Spiritually governed
- Chemically/hormonally driven
- Biologically/physically carried out.

• •

Dawn Breslin

The key to me feeling amazing is in allowing myself to do nothing when I have so much to do.

• •

Jane Alexander

Like most forty-something women, I'm a juggler. I write about holistic health and contemporary spirituality while also trying my hardest to be a good enough mother, wife, daughter, friend … If there's any time left over I try to spend it trimming my body and expanding my soul. If I could be a deity, I'd definitely like to be a Hindu one with a few extra pairs of hands!

My very first memory is of a hedge – dark leaves with hundreds of tiny cocoons. My mother was amazed as apparently that hedge was cut down when I was about eight months old. Now I think about it, it's a pretty telling memory as all my life I have sought ways to go within and transform, so the cocoon has been (and still is) a powerful symbol for me. I truly believe that if we want to grow there will be times when we have to dissolve and almost 'break down' first. Spirituality isn't all about being light and bright – there are also dark nights of the soul, and very necessary they are too.

Having said that, I also think it's important to see the positive on a day-to-day basis. Every night before I go to sleep, I make a list of ten things I'm grateful for from the day that has just been. It always makes me smile (and sometimes cry too) and is the one practice I recommend to everyone as it has the capacity to banish depression, anxiety and envy like nothing else. It makes you focus on what you have already got, rather than what you think you want. It brings you into the present and makes you see the bright side of life. It also makes you realize that – on the whole – it's people, not possessions, that are important. I never find I am particularly grateful for that pair of smart shoes, or that new necklace. But I *am* hugely grateful for my family, my health, a roof over my head and the beauty of the world around me. I'm also grateful for the little things that make life special – the leaves turning colour, a new waterfall appearing after heavy rain, a warm dog curled up on my lap, a small boy hurling himself into my arms, a gentle kiss from my husband. Those are the things that make me happiest.

Massage is my secret pampering treat – I love any form of hands-on bodywork but my favourites are Chavutti

Thirumal, Thai massage, Tragerwork and any form of deep-tissue work. I look on it as mind work as much as body work – memories and pain (both physical and emotional) are stored in the muscles, fascia and bone, and can be teased out with good massage or manipulation. It's like therapy without having to say a word.

• •

Deepak Chopra

Ten Keys to Happiness

1. Listen to your body's wisdom, which expresses itself through signals of comfort and discomfort. When choosing a certain behaviour, ask your body, 'How do you feel about this?' If your body sends a signal of physical or emotional distress, watch out. If your body sends a signal of comfort and eagerness, proceed.

2. Live in the present, for it is the only moment you have. Keep your attention on what is here and now; look for the fullness in every moment. Accept what comes to you totally and completely so that you can appreciate it, learn from it, and then let it go. The present is as it should be. It reflects infinite laws of Nature that have brought you this exact thought, this exact physical response. This moment is as it is because the universe is as it is. Don't struggle against the infinite scheme of things; instead, be at one with it.

3. Take time to be silent, to meditate, to quieten the internal dialogue. In moments of silence, realize that you are recontacting your source of pure awareness. Pay attention to your inner life so that you can be guided by intuition rather than externally imposed interpretations of what is or isn't good for you.

4. Relinquish your need for external approval. You alone are the judge of your worth, and your goal is to discover infinite worth in yourself, no matter what anyone else thinks. There is great freedom in this realization.

5. When you find yourself reacting with anger or opposition to any person or circumstance, realize that you are only struggling with yourself. Putting up resistance is the response of defences created by old hurts. When you relinquish this anger, you will be healing yourself and co-operating with the flow of the universe.

6. Know that the world 'out there' reflects your reality 'in here'. The people you react to most strongly, whether with love or hate, are projections of your inner world. What you most hate is what you most deny in yourself. What you most love is what you most wish for in yourself. Use the mirror of relationships to guide your evolution. The goal is total self-knowledge. When you achieve that, what you most want will automatically be there, and what you most dislike will disappear.

7. Shed the burden of judgement – you will feel much lighter. Judgement imposes right and wrong on situations that just are. Everything can be understood and forgiven; but when you judge, you cut off understanding and shut down the process of learning to love. In judging others, you reflect your lack of self-acceptance. Remember that every person you forgive adds to your self-love.

8. Don't contaminate your body with toxins, whether through food, drink or toxic emotions. Your body is more than a life-support system. It is the vehicle that will carry you on the journey of your evolution. The health of every cell directly contributes to your state of wellbeing, because every cell is a point of awareness within the field of awareness that is you.

9. Replace fear-motivated behaviour with love-motivated behaviour. Fear is the product of memory, which dwells in the past. By remembering what hurt us before, we direct our energies toward making certain that an old hurt will not repeat itself. But trying to impose the past on the present can never wipe out the threat of being hurt. That happens only when you find the security of your own being, which is love. Motivated by the truth inside you, you can face any threat because your inner strength is invulnerable to fear.

10. Understand that the physical world is just a mirror of a deeper intelligence. Intelligence is the invisible

organizer of all matter and energy, and since a portion of this intelligence resides in you, you share in the organising power of the cosmos. Because you are inseparably linked to everything, you cannot afford to foul the planet's air and water. But at a deeper level, you cannot afford to live with a toxic mind, because every thought makes an impression on the whole field of intelligence. Living in balance and purity is the highest good for you and the Earth.

● ●

Sarah Bartlett

Q *Sun sign and other planetary influences?*

A Gemini with a crazy moon/Uranus conjunction in Cancer, square to a Saturn and Neptune conjunction in Libra, opposite Chiron.

There are many bits of me – good qualities, shadowy ones – as with every individual. One I will share is the moon/Uranus set-up in my chart which reveals I'm a freedom lover. I hate feeling fenced-in and like variety in what I do. I'm restless, and hate domesticity, routines and roots. There's one side of me which does want to belong, to have a home and security, but another which just has to get up and go somewhere else. The moon wants to belong, to attach itself to someone or something; Uranus doesn't. Add that to an equally restless Gemini sun, and a travel-loving Sagittarius ascendant and you can imagine that I'm harder to catch than a mosquito.

The way I deal with this is to live a pretty unconventional life. I became an astrologer because astrology is full of polarities and that is the fundamental nature of the moon/Uranus theme. I am, quite simply, a lover of paradox.

Q *Most treasured possession?*

A I treasure my ragged old puppet doll with no face called Gulliver. He was given to me by an ancient magus, an aged professor I used to call Doctor Fear, who lived in a big spooky house on the outskirts of Cambridge that I visited with my parents when I was six. I think he gave Gulliver to me because he knew I was a kindred spirit. Gulliver is very bizarre, but he holds the secret of all secrets in his invisible gaze. When you look at him you see what you want to see. He is a mirror for your own truth. He's travelled with me extensively.

Q *What do you know about where society is heading?*

A Future secrets? Well, I could ask Gulliver! But he would probably say that the future is the biggest secret going, so why not just let it reveal itself? Secrets and mysteries are there to baffle us, to make us think, to seek answers or truths for ourselves. And the way you go about discovering a secret says more about you than it does about the secret. But that doesn't necessarily mean we are obliged to discover the truth. The invisible is simply that. But we swirl in anxiety about discovering what the future holds. Perhaps it's better to accept that the hidden is hidden. The unknown is unknown, and secrets will always be secrets.

Yet we go on seeking the answers, because if we know a secret that someone else doesn't know, we immediately have some kind of power. And that is a very dangerous thing, especially in the professions like astrology which, on the surface, apparently 'look to the future'.

Astrology looks at any moment in time whether in the past, present or future. And that moment only mirrors the potential of that moment, not necessarily what is manifest. So, back to original question: no, I don't know where we're heading, but I do believe that we journey along the road that we make for ourselves. That is the secret.

. . . .

Fiona Harrold

What makes me happiest is people fulfilling their potential and taking responsibility for their own happiness. Because when people do that it makes for a much happier world, where people are taking responsibility rather than blaming other people or waiting for a government or an individual to change things for them. When people sort their lives out they are then in a position to make a contribution to others and the world at large. If people are impoverished and full of loathing for their life they're not in a great state to make a contribution to anyone, including themselves. I love it when people straighten out their lives and do the things they should be doing. It's a neat way to live.

My mantra is 'I'll handle it.' It takes away any fear that ever arises from me about my life. Any time I suddenly think about the bills coming in, or whatever it is, I immediately quieten that fear or horror by reminding myself that I'll handle it. Whatever happens, whatever the situation – I'll handle it.

HEALTH & HEALING SECRETS

Susan Phoenix

One night, I awoke to feel the most amazing energetic force-field around my body. It was as if a loving partner was hugging me warmly. This was not physically possible at the time because my husband had been killed three years previously. When I began to relax and understand this phenomenon I realized that it was another energy interacting with my own. How wonderful to know that the soul's energy can continue to make itself known in times of need (I was severely depressed at the time).

For me this was the beginning of my research into energy fields. I'd experienced Angelic presence whilst studying ascension techniques with Diana Cooper but I had not really thought about the scientific reasons for such vibrations in our environment. Of course everything in our life is an energetic force of some form – all those vibrating molecules that we learned about in school are now coming into their own. The Universe is definitely trying to communicate with this New Age and is ready to bypass the traditional channels of mediums and psychics by allowing us all to feel and eventually to see for ourselves.

I was told by my husband's spirit to produce 'evidence' for the world to grasp this beautiful energy field around us that can communicate so much for our benefit. The aura camera was one of the first tools that I could use to show how the human energy field can absorb peripheral energies from other people, crystals and essential oils.

Also, more surprisingly, by calling in the energy of a loved one or pure angelic energy from the 'other dimensions', we can change our own auras. What beautiful changes are produced and recorded by cameras and receptors in the auric field when this happens. The spirit presence from loved ones passed over is often seen as a white ball effect or occasionally an elongated shape next to the client. Different angels create different colours – Archangel Michael has a beautiful blue ray, while the healing green ray of Archangel Raphael often shows in aura photos when people need more physical healing.

If someone does not have the faith to call in outside energies for themselves it is a pleasure to watch their surprise when they have a second aura photograph taken after a five-minute healing session or a short meditation. The aura absorbs the relaxing vibrations provided by the cosmos and the blood pressure is also lowered accordingly. Holistic health recorded at its best.

One of my dreams is to allow the people of the world access to their own soul's healing powers as they learn to interact with the other dimensions in safety and peace without chemical intervention or fear.

Hamilton Harris

**Secret way of pampering or healing yourself that
makes you feel amazing**

CARNATION AND CINNAMON
CLEANSING BATH

Ingredients:

- Ten white carnations
- Florida water
- Rose petal water
- Cinnamon powder

1. Fill the bath halfway with water to suit body
   temperature.

2. Remove the rose head from the stem and scatter
   petals on the water.

3. Add Florida and rose water and four tablespoons
   of cinnamon to the bath.

4. Leave to marinate for five minutes.

5. Light a pink candle for healing visualisation as
   you immerse your body head to toe, cleansing
   your energies and healing yourself.

Gloria Thomas

There has never been a time such as now when people have become disconnected from their true selves. Most of this is caused by the conditioning of our Western culture. We are not educated about the power and potential of our minds. The effect of this is a complete lack of communication with the larger part, which is unconscious. This lack of awareness has resulted in disharmony in mind, body and spirit in epidemic proportions. Yet that power and potential is there to be tapped into.

One of my favorite tools is a natural skill, although I didn't know it till late, that never fails to astound and amaze me – my intuition.

Neuro Linguistic Programming teaches us that we all have the same neurology, so that what one person can do, so can another. With this revelation in mind, and a long fascination with psychic studies, I decided to learn how mystics and mediums do what they do.

Only 7% of our communication is words – 38% is tonality and 55% is body language. So I set out to find how to use my senses to tune in, like a radio, to what is going on beneath the surface of an individual's state of mind or physical condition.

I would ask myself what else I needed to know that would give me information to inform this person's process for transformation or healing. Through meditative practices and by tuning into the different chakras (energy centres of the body) information comes in words, pictures and feelings.

It gives both the client and me remarkable insight into what is really going on. Such clarity helps enormously with change, transformation and healing. In discovering this simple skill, I wondered – what else can we tap into that can help and support our growth and healing? Possibly a great deal ...

Samantha Hamilton

COLOUR RAY OF LIGHTS MEDITATION TO CLEAR THE CHAKRAS AND HEAL THE BODY

1. Find yourself somewhere comfortable and quiet to sit – switch off the phone. Close your eyes and envisage yourself in a temple, walking out into a garden in beautiful surroundings with a crystal blue stream running by you. The sky is a clear blue and a bright warm sun is shining down on you with a soft breeze gently swirling.

2. Envisage the angel of healing, Raphael. Feel the presence of the angel healing you with an abundance of colour from the rainbow.

3. Select a colour you feel drawn to for your self-healing. To help decide, visualize a rainbow of colour all around you and feel the seven colours of the spectrum. Choose the colour you're most drawn to as your guide for this meditation.

4. Now see white clouds in the clear blue sky above you. Imagine yourself floating within them. Choose one of these clouds and fill it with your inner healing energies; feel this cloud become you. Start to see this cloud sparkling with light and feel its warm energy.

5. Visualize Raphael embracing you above the clouds

and holding you as you become immersed by the healing energies of your chosen colour.

6. Feel the breeze caressing your skin, moving around you and enveloping you. It becomes a part of you, like second skin, and cleanses your bloodstream. The healing vibration allows you to move completely into a deeply relaxed state of being.

7. Allow this colour to flow through your body for at least five minutes more, giving you a feeling of wholeness.

8. Allow the pores of your skin to open to the healing, releasing toxins.

9. Now self-healed, stay quietly with your cleared mind, body and soul for a few minutes. Take in three deep breaths, releasing each breath with peace, before opening your eyes.

Kate West

A friend of mine had been sick for a long time and was being referred to a specialist in tropical medicine. Although she hadn't asked for healing, my partner and I worked a spell that same night.

In the Circle, we carved a blue candle with the name and birth sign of our subject. We then anointed it with lavender oil and lit it. As it burnt down we visualized healing passing to my friend and driving out all disease.

The following morning my friend's symptoms had completely gone.

• •

William Bloom

THE SOUL IN ITS TEMPLE
MEDITATION

This is a meditation that I do several times a day, but especially when I wake up and before I go to sleep.

Sit or lie in any position. Just be comfortable and relaxed as best you can.

Soften your eyes.
Open your heart.
Turn your focus down into your own body.

Especially, let your chest and lower stomach relax and sink.

Lower your eyes slightly, as if looking down into your body.
Like an affectionate friend taking care of a small child, scan how your body feels.
Be friendly and caring towards your body.
Use your best bedside manner.
Greet any tension or ache with acceptance and friendship.

This sends crucial messages through the nervous system so that endorphins are triggered, tissue opens and the body's healing agents can work effectively.

From a spiritual perspective, using traditional language, this helps your soul – your compassionate, core consciousness – to land and incarnate into its temple, your physical body.

● ●

Cassandra Eason

This is something I use for myself when I have bad gall-bladder pain, often while travelling when I have to miss meals or eat snacks. I also used it to soothe my children and draw pain like earache or headaches from them, though I have never told them. I regularly apply this to my oldest cat, Jenny, who now is nearly 18 and very creaky, but hates vets.

First I touch near or on the place of pain or discomfort with the fingertips of my power hand, the one I write with. Then I hold up my power hand, with palm vertical, fingers together and facing outwards and very gently push away into the air.

I say in my mind, 'Go from me, flow from me [or I name the person], leave only harmony.' People just think I am gesturing as I am talking, but it really floats away the pain.

• •

Caroline Shola Arewa

Creating EASE

The secret I want to share with you has emerged from more than 20 years working in spiritual and personal development. I have come to understand that, *if you are not creating ease in your life, you are creating dis-ease.*

I have grown increasingly passionate about helping people to create success without stress. For this reason I developed a four-step energy-based approach to balanced living.

CREATING EASE – A FOUR-STEP APPROACH TO MASTERING ENERGY AND AWARENESS TO CREATE SUCCESS AND EXCELLENCE

1. Everything is made of **Energy**, including you.

Energy flows through chakras, which distribute energy throughout your body. When energy is depleted you experience tiredness, fatigue, stress and dis-ease. Balanced energy brings health, happiness and success. How do you use and abuse your energy?

2. Awareness

Creating EASE asks you to heighten your awareness and balance activity with rest. Stop thinking that success requires hard work and long hours. It doesn't. Take it easy. Fast, fearful and fatigued is not the best way. It only causes energy drain, resulting in burnout, stress and dis-ease. I suggest, and science supports, taking more time for rest and recovery. Less is more. What must you change to enhance your wellbeing?

3. Success

Life has an assignment just for you; it's your Divine Purpose. To successfully complete your assignment you need to:

- use energy efficiently
- develop personal awareness
- develop awareness of universal power
- exercise faith.

These qualities move you towards greater success. An infinite intelligence works through you and when you trust its power everything is possible. You can embrace success whenever you choose.

4. **Excellence** comes after the earlier steps are achieved, like reaching the crest of a mountain.

Excellence develops as a result of properly managed energy and awareness. It helps you create your best self, best work and best life.

When more energy is moving you forward than holding you back, success is in your grasp. You have the opportunity to work with the universal power that governs you to create your unique destiny. Each breath you take and every move you make determine your future. What are you creating right now in your life? Remember: if you are not creating EASE you are creating dis-ease!

William Bloom

This wonderful meditation embeds in your body what some people call the 'bliss fields' or the 'Cosmic Christ' or 'Nirvana'. It is part of my daily practice and I see it as being crucial for my health and for keeping me consciously connected to the wonder of all existence.

HEALING MEDITATION – EMBEDDING THE CONNECTION

Sit quietly, waiting until you have settled into stillness. Sometimes this may take up to 20 minutes, but just wait patiently, allowing the mind to do its stuff and then guiding it into being relaxed and calm.

To begin with, keep your focus completely inside your body, noticing how you feel. Gently allow your mind to become compassionate, watchful and caring. Open your heart and do your best to develop an attitude and an energy that are loving.

Then allow yourself to be aware of the vastness of space – above you, to your sides and below you. Be aware of yourself on Earth – and that Earth is floating in space. Be aware of the solar system. The galaxy. The whole cosmos and outwards into infinity.

Stay relaxed in your body, well-grounded and centred.

Then allow every cell in your body to become like a receptive sponge or radar dish, allowing in the healing vitality and benevolence that permeate the cosmos. Allow every cell in your body to feel and sense the wonder of all existence. Experience this as a tangible energy field that penetrates all aspects of your body and psyche. Let this sensation of benevolence sink deep in, down into the bone marrow, spinal cord and brain tissue.

Do this for as long as feels comfortable. Then make sure your awareness and focus are fully in your body. Become centred and grounded. Stretch and move on.

DIET AND EXERCISE TIPS

······································

William Bloom

Starting the day with a pint of warm water is very good for me and for most people. I avoid breakfast and eat only after I've been up and moving for two hours.

At the risk of sounding obvious, the real tip about exercise is actually to exercise! Do it! Don't think about it!

This means keeping your body moving all through the day from the moment you wake up. We were not designed to slob about or sit at a desk all day. Minimally, move around for at least an hour a day even if it is just doing the housework. I see housework as an opportunity for exercise! It needs doing with a good attitude too. If you work at a desk, get up and stretch and stroll every thirty minutes.

Another great tip is to be stretching just when you're walking. Anyone who has done yoga, qi gung or Alexander technique will know that it is the sense of *expansion* in your body tissue that matters. So try walking around with a sense that every part of your body is opening up and expanding.

Also keep your exercise balanced, blending aerobic,

stretching and weights. I go to the gym twice a week and stretch every day. Caring for my body absolutely enhances the quality of my life.

• •

Jane Alexander

My best exercise tip is to invest in a rebounder – a small trampoline – and plonk it in front of your television. Bounce to the news, your favourite soap, or during the ads. Bouncing is great aerobic exercise, is gentle on your joints and stimulates the lymphatic system, so it's good stuff. It's also great fun – which is essential for any exercise regime you want to stand the test of time!

• •

Laura Berridge

Have a food-tolerance test and combine it with knowledge of the Ayurvedic dosha system, then buy only food that works for you.

–   Select 50 or so basic yet favourite compatible recipes from cookery books so there are always easy and enjoyable healthy meals to eat without stress, and less tendency to eat junk or sweets.

- Monitor regular meals and portions to keep the body's energy and metabolism consistent.

- Only exercise in ways which bring joy, otherwise you're giving yourself negative messages, which is where problems begin.

• •

Jon Sandifer

From the age of 23 I began to practise macrobiotics. I had travelled round some 52 countries, eating the local foods, predominantly in developing countries, making the connection between eating local seasonal foods and feeling in tune with my environment. Macrobiotics embraced the same principle. I still enjoy macrobiotic quality foods, such as brown rice, beans, sea vegetables, miso, fish, pickles and seasonal fruits – but what I really learnt, and still appreciate, is the importance of chewing.

The whole digestive process begins in the mouth and if you do not take the time to chew your food well, you obviously do not digest it very well either. That same principle can also be applied as a metaphor for life. Simply speaking, it means don't rush into anything. Chew it really well. If you hear a new idea, chew it before you undertake it. Sometimes we come across something that we do not necessarily agree with on face value, but if you chew it well, in a metaphorical sense, then maybe you will find something of value there.

Judi James

I should write a book about dieting! I am now 5'9" and a size eight but I struggled with my weight throughout a long modelling career, so I really have been there and done it.

The only good diet is no diet. The emotional pressures of 'being on a diet' are enormous, far too great to cope with. It also suggests the idea to your subconscious that you are either 'on' or 'off' a diet, which leads to binge eating. I only lost weight when I stopped dieting.

I eat for health now, so there are no good or bad days, I just eat what I know is good for me. It's amazing how quickly the obsession with food drops away. I stopped weighing myself when I stopped dieting too. The scales can also become obsessional.

The key problem with slimmers is that they have no true idea of their actual goal. If you're going to achieve great things in life you must always know what that goal looks like before you start. Slimmers think they just want to be slim but they don't, which is why they often end up piling weight back on again. Slimmers want to be thin but eat whatever and as much as they like, that's their real goal; I know because I've been there. Thin isn't enough, we want to be thin people who can eat loads and never put on a pound.

Either change your way of thinking, stop worrying about

the extra pounds and enjoy eating what you want, or make your life more busy, buzzy and full of adrenalin to burn up the calories faster – and fill your life with other concerns.

● ●

Fiona Harrold

Making your life work well and keeping it exciting and interesting are the most important staying-in-shape secret that I know of. Often it's not a diet that we need, it's actually changing our life, improving it in some way. We often overeat out of boredom and unhappiness, and then food is nothing to do with hunger but filling up a sense of irritation or emptiness. Replenishing ourselves and nourishing ourselves with an exciting life, full of challenges, to stretch ourselves and create adrenalin, are the best thing to do to keep in shape, rather than obsessing about food.

Simon Brown

Healing with the energy of food

Emotional energy called chi runs through all our bodies. It changes according to the time of day, the weather and especially the food we eat. While the nutritional content of food is obviously important, it's also worth taking into account the living energy of what you eat. Any food you put in your mouth changes your energy from the inside, where shiatsu or acupuncture might change the energy from the outside.

Look at the direction the food grows, how it lives and how it's cooked.

Eat leafy green vegetables that grow upwards to help move your energy up, and into the chest and mind. Root vegetables grow downwards, so they move energy down and into your intestines and legs.

Then look at where a food is in its life cycle. Anything right at the beginning, such as wholegrains, nuts and seeds would have a very vibrant, curious, youthful energy. Ancient foods such as shellfish and sea vegetables have a vital, primal energy.

More mature food, fully grown vegetables, meat and fish will have the energy of experience and survival instinct. Chicken would give a quick, alert but nervy energy while wild salmon, which swims upstream, will give you that sense of going against the grain and finding your own path in life. Eat something that has roamed the countryside and you'll pick up an ability to deal with challenges as they come.

The emotion the animal goes through when it's being killed is important. If it's unpleasant, any stress and fear might still be in the meat to be passed on to you when you eat it. So organic is always preferable to farmed.

How you prepare the food also makes a big difference to its energy. Steaming is an up energy. Baking and pressure cooking would give you more of an inner strength. Stewing brings energy down. Frying helps spread energy outwards.

So fried garlic, ginger and onions, because they also grow outwards, would make you feel your energy was coming to the surface quicker. For instant energy, a mixture of fried and steamed food would be best. Try fried rice or noodles with ginger, garlic and some mild spices, with steamed green veg. Great to have before a meeting where you need extra oomph. For a more long-lasting energy, a simple stew, with root vegetables, pressure-cooked brown rice, or porridge would be better.

Following this approach, you can bring more healing energy into the body. With any intestinal problem try root vegetable and stews to give a warm feeling in your abdomen and slowly get things moving. To open the chest and get rid of heaviness during a cold or even asthma, try vibrant foods that push up and out, such as miso soup with green vegetables and ginger. Apply it to anything for total wellbeing.

• •

Silja

Diet tricks

If you wish to lose weight, start any diet or exercise regime just after a full moon, so that as the moon gets smaller, your waist will too!

Drinking a cup of green tea before every meal acts as a natural appetite suppressant. Plus green tea is packed with super-nutrients and it burns calories.

Lighting a slim white candle and having it burning while you eat will help too. If you feel tempted to eat that chocolate bar, or feel you just must finish what's on your plate despite not being hungry any more, look at the candle flame and imagine how much healthier and happier you will be when you get fitter.

BEAUTY SECRETS

· ·

Lucy Lam

Sun signs' inner beauty tips

In my years as an astrologer and agony aunt, I have seen
that lack of confidence and low self-esteem can be caused
by losing a sense of your sun sign. A 'missing' sun sign
causes a lack of identity. So if you're a Scorpio who feels
drab or a less than radiant Leo, take action to reveal your
inner self and reach true happiness. Here's how:

Aries: You crave adrenalin, and need to capture a
natural blush in your cheeks by exciting heart-in-your-
mouth activities. Go-karting, parachuting, anything
speed-driven and competitive will make you sparkle,
inside and out.

Taurus: Indulge yourself with sensuous massage – receiving, but giving's good too. Go for walks in lush countryside, nibble on mouth-watering foods and wear nature-
inspired scents. Wonderful love-making is your ultimate
beautifier.

Gemini: Become your quicksilver best by communicating your feelings with youthful, witty friends. Laughter is
one of the greatest beauty therapies for you. Even
exercise should be fun – and in a group, so you can social-
ize too.

Cancer: If your shell has become so hard that you cannot access your deep emotions, have a day when you allow yourself to feel joy, sadness and love. Plan special experiences with family or friends, watch weepy, feel-good films or listen to rousing music.

Leo: Creativity is your oxygen, so make sure you're expressing yourself, even if it's just goofing around with the kids. Dance, drama and singing make you feel wonderful, even better if there's an audience. A back massage makes you purr with delight.

Virgo: If you've become disorganized and slobbish, get yourself a project you can be in control of – even if it's just getting your garden in order. Don't neglect your health, eat wholefoods, get plenty of fresh air, exercise and try yoga or relaxation techniques to help stop worrying.

Libra: You need harmonious surroundings and people around you, so seek these out. Indulge your sense of romance – even if you don't have a lover, pay homage to your body with candle-lit, petal-strewn baths, and slather on fragrant lotions afterwards.

Scorpio: When you're on form your natural charisma attracts others to you, so sorting out your feelings with some kind of therapy could be a magical beautifier. Try swimming and kickboxing to purge you of any negativity. Tantalize your taste buds with spicy treats and curries. Sex is a real invigorator for you too!

Sagittarius: Feeling stifled and bored will make you feel dull and jaded, so cram your life full of action, challenge and fun. Nourish your mind with new experiences and philosophies. Get regular, exciting sex – or get your highs from adrenaline-boosting activities such as skydiving or abseiling.

Capricorn: If you're out of control of yourself, whether it's your emotions or your body, you won't be happy. Get regular massages or osteopathy. You need to work hard to be happy – but make sure this is balanced by rest and recharging your mind, body and spirit.

Aquarius: If you're blending into the crowd instead of leading it, allow your true, original self – and beauty – to shine through. New-age activities like rebirthing or Bikram yoga, plus exhilarating winter sports, will put colour in your cheeks. Even the sex you have should be tantric!

Pisces: If the big, bad world has made you lose your soft, ethereal beauty, you need to reclaim your inner sensitivity. Get spiritual and meditate. Use aromatic bath oils to soothe and lift your spirits. Try gentle exercise such as swimming or tai chi.

Inbaal

I am a Piscean, so am naturally a starry-eyed romantic who believes in love at first sight, true love and perfect soulmates. But I have a Sagittarius moon which accounts for my clumsy streak and absolute inability to be graceful and sexy under any circumstances. I once tried to go all gothic for a Hallowe'en do. Black lipstick, slicked-back hair, black lace gloves, the lot. I looked like Dracula's younger brother. Any 5'1", curvaceous girl who's a natural F cup that can look like a man in drag deserves a round of applause!

My ascendant is Libra, which is awful on the one hand, because I love beautiful people. I realize it's judgemental and unkind, but on the other hand, this Libra rising thing makes me want to make people beautiful. When I once worked in retail, I always knew intuitively how to put people in the clothes that make the most of what they've got.

Essentially, I believe everyone has a latent beauty and that happy people are inherently beautiful. A lovely phenomenon I like to observe is people's growth into themselves. Some of my clients come for a reading every year, or every couple of years. As they implement various changes and self-improvements into their lives, and as they learn to affirm that which they are and that which they long to be, they become more comfortable in their own skins. Their faces de-crease, their brows de-furrow, posture and motion gain their own grace, and in front of me stands a person resplendent in their uniqueness.

For those who are not this positive all the time, it's always worth trying a little magic:

On Friday (Venus's day, Goddess of Love and Beauty) of a full moon, light a blue (health, the only thing more important than beauty) candle after rubbing rosemary (for sleep, can't be beautiful when tired!) on it, and look in the mirror in the light of that candle. See your wrinkles smoothing, your features enhancing, see yourself as your most Beautiful Self.

• •

Jon Sandifer

I was born and raised in Kenya. My earliest memory, as a child aged about three, is of brushing my teeth like the locals.

My parents had bought me some kind of toothpaste and a toothbrush, but the African housemaid, whose job it was to wash and dress me in the morning, would have none of it. I remember walking around the tropical garden shortly after dawn every morning with her. She would take me to a secluded area, well out of view of the house, and we would sit underneath a gigantic shrub of a lemon tree. She would break off a couple of twigs from the tree, peel back the bark and reveal the glistening white inner core of the twig. This was her toothbrush.

She taught me at this early age that toothbrushes and toothpaste were a complete waste of time, and that rubbing your teeth and gums vigorously every morning with this pithy sap was the best thing to do, but never tell your parents! To this day I'm still blessed with good teeth and gums, thanks to her.

• •

Silja

Magical soak:

I add a few drops of vanilla essential oil (calming, self-assuring) to almond oil (assists with success and feeling beautiful) to the running water.

Beauty rituals:

Sparkling face powder can be used in a magical beauty ritual. To gain the mysteriousness and mischievous fun of the pixies, add a few drops of water from a fast-flowing stream and a few fern seeds to your sparkly powder before applying. Make sure to re-apply at midnight for an extra boost to your allure!

If you feel you are on the rebound or just too laden with trouble from work, this can negatively influence your drawing power when going on a date. To counteract that, make a rub with oats (to gain the power of the Moon Goddess), salt (to dispel any negativity) and a few drops of vanilla essence (to draw love to you). Then rub your whole body with it before a shower.

Having a really bad day at work or with your family? Draw a warm bath and add a few drops of geranium essential oil to it, as well as three teaspoons of vinegar. Swirl the water counter-clockwise with your left hand, then step into the water and make sure you submerge yourself fully at least once.

Bringing the Goddess into daily life:

There are many ways to gently remind yourself of the power of Mother Earth in your life and bring Goddess energy into your everyday activities. You don't need to enact big rituals!

When you wake up in the morning, instead of grumpily throwing the covers aside, take three deep breaths and think of one nice thing you plan on doing today, one thing to look forward to. Even the dullest day will look brighter!

Try to eat organic fruit and veg whenever you can. When you are using eggs in the kitchen, look out for double-yolked ones: they are the portent of unexpected good luck! At work, consider having a round-leaf plant on your desk; not only will it give extra oxygen, it will also encourage positive interactions and draw money to you.

SECTION THREE

LOVE; SENSUAL, SEXUAL SECRETS;
SPELLS & SIGNS, CHARMS & CHANTS;
HOME; EARTH

Emma Restall Orr

Q *Sun sign and other planetary influences*

A I am hopelessly Scorpio, the core of my life having always been within the realms of sexuality, sensuality, intensity, decay, death and regeneration. Yet in many ways this explains the focus of my work, in a religious tradition that is based upon deep connection and reverence for the forces of nature. What could be more central to life than sex and death, after all? What allows me to work publicly and share the tradition, through teaching and ritual, writing and the media, is the Leo in me (moon in Leo and Leo rising), although the blend is sometimes a little alarming ...

Q *Favourite thing about what you do*

A My work as a priest is so completely integrated into my life as a human being that it is hard to think of it in terms of what I do, for it is more about what I am. However, in saying that, I am expressing perhaps the most poignant and beautiful part of my work: that it doesn't require me to be anything but myself.

Q *First memory*

A When I was three my family lived in Denmark. My earliest negative memories are of being trapped on the ceiling, looking down at my body in bed, crying out for help and nobody hearing my soundless voice.

My earliest positive memories are of snow in the forest, the overwhelming sensation of a brilliant and glowing pure white on the ground, many feet thick with a surface that crunched under my boots, and the dark pine canopy above. I had no doubt in that moment that the forest was a profoundly magical place, and that sense of wonder has remained with me ever since.

Q *What makes you smile a secret smile or makes you happiest?*

A The simplicity of life. As human beings, we have a ridiculous capacity to complicate moments or relationships. So remembering that life is utterly simple makes me smile. And it's no ordinary smile: it floods through every part of me, with relief, release and the laughter that comes when the road lies clear and open once again before me.

Q *Top tip for meditation*

A The idea that meditation is about emptying the mind is, to me, a misdirection. In Druidry, meditation is about becoming entirely involved in a single relationship. For the period of time put aside, whether it be just a minute or an hour or more, with perfect acceptance, without demands, without communication, we sit together in peace.

Some of the easiest relationships to focus on for any length of time are the waves of the sea, the flow of a river, a flickering hearth fire, or the sun as it sets. With all these we can spend a long time simply being; our minds may drift into daydreams, but our meditation is effective if we hold our attention, just watching, listening, breathing in the scent, nothing more.

Q *Favourite place in the world?*

A I couldn't possibly choose, for different moments call for different environments. A gathering of three ancient yews, the nearby stone circle, various beautiful trees in the forest, my local graveyard, my garden ... However, the most truthful answer is probably now the embrace of my husband. Curled up together, we lose our edges, our spirits merging, and that is by far the most peaceful and beautiful place I regularly go to.

Q *Deep beliefs that keep you going when things are tough*

A That there is no beginning and no end. In Druidry, the image given in the old Celtic knotwork, much of which is based on more ancient designs, is of a flow of life that has no starting point and no finish. The thread simply winds its way under and over other threads, in swirls and loops, implying circles and spirals. The knotwork reflects the deep belief that many Druids hold, that there was no moment in which the universe was created and there will be no apocalyptic end.

Life emerges and recedes, lifetimes come and go; songs rise out of the hum of life, coming into form through sound, then dissolve back into the songs of nature.

It is a belief that allows a strong sense of presence, of being awake and alive, here and now, instead of reaching into the future or getting stuck in the past. It allows us to let go of what is done and, having learned from the experience, walk with our feet on the ground, every step lightly taken, with respect and responsibility. It enables us to feel the continuity of life, knowing that every action we take affects that continuity. It helps us to remember that all of nature is connected.

Q *Who or what inspires you most and why?*

A Within humanity, it is music. For music is such a powerful expression of human nature, communicating grief and joy, community and tribal pride, energy and determination, glory and humility. Music has been a part of human culture for longer than we can ever know, with our distant ancestors dancing to the drums, singing to the spirits of nature. We still do it. Festivals like Glastonbury or Live8 reveal how essential that community experience of music is. In Druidry, music and dance are a key part of many individuals' spiritual practice. Certainly I sing and dance all the time!

Beyond humanity, in the worlds within which we live, what inspires me is simply nature's incredible creativity. Take a walk, anywhere, in city streets or country woodland, and you'll find the most beautiful expressions of nature: tender flower petals, intricate cobwebs, birdsong, plants growing out of the tiniest cracks, havens of life under logs, the patterns of trees against the skies …

Q *Secret fantasy to make the world a better place?*

A Fair trade.

It may not sound like a secret, for we all know that fair trade is the only way that there can be honourable exchange between seller and buyer. Yet in reality the percentage of goods that are fairly traded is tiny. There are millions of people around the world growing coffee, tea, cocoa, sugar, cotton and so on, who are receiving so little for their goods that they are making a loss, while the multinationals that retail these products in the West are making enormous profits. It's wrong.

Yet we can't simply blame the big companies. We may only vote once every four or five years for a government, but we vote every day with every penny we spend. The majority are still voting for poverty caused by unfair trade. If every reader of this book only ever bought fair-trade coffee, tea, chocolate, bananas etc., it would make a huge difference. If every citizen of Britain did, life would change for millions of people.

Q *Sensual, sexual secrets*

A Some already tell us that our physical bodies are not the most sensuous parts of us: our mind is. And indeed we can add to our physical pleasure with fantasies, expectations, imagination and so on. However, in Druidry, the body and the mind are not seen as separate parts of us. It is understood that what heightens our pleasure is the play of energy between us.

Foreplay should always begin without touching. Holding ourselves a few inches apart, feeling our lover so close yet without any physical contact, we can sense each other's energy. The tingle of life, of anticipation, can be exquisitely erotic. Moving from that point to skin on skin has to be gentle, tentative, a whisper of breath, the brush of a fingertip, a lock of hair, even if passion comes flooding in and brings our love-making into wildly physical interaction later.

But let that be later ... Intimacy without touch is worth exploring.

Q *If you could be a deity, who would you be and why?*

A I would be a goddess of rain. Rain is the most exquisitely sensual power of nature, for it can seep into all we are, exploring every crack and curve, sliding down skin and rock and petal, playing upon rivers and pools, making music on rooftops, springing the softest drops of mist, thundering down, feeding the dry soil with the power of potential life.

And what a powerful force, what a gift and a weapon it is. If I were a goddess of rain, perhaps I would have some compassion, and offer water where it was needed, and hold back where it was not. As a human being, that kind of philanthropy is appealing. But as a priest of nature, a Druid, I have no sense that a rain goddess has that sense of care. She is simply rain: wild, free and filled with song.

LOVE SECRETS

Brian Bates

The Way of Wyrd

Inspirational secrets are of two kinds. There are those that are hidden away from our knowing in remote times and places like ancient manuscripts, or in cloud-hidden mountain retreats in places like Tibet. Then there are the other kind that are right in front of our noses every day, but which we fail to see because they are too obvious.

The secrets of The Way of Wyrd are of both these kinds. I found many of them in an ancient manuscript written over one thousand years ago by a monk in a stone monastery in Anglo-Saxon England. On leaves of parchment he recorded not Christian doctrine, but the healing secrets of wizards from that ancient culture. This precious document is now in the British Library.

When I studied it, I discovered many lost inspirations recorded there. Behind them all was one profound truth. It is the very elixir of life. It is love.

We all know about love, of course, and it seems so obvious that surely we should be looking elsewhere for 'secrets'. Yet I think this is the most powerful secret of all, and it is the place to start. We all seek love. We seek it in personal relationships, in our families, in world peace.

But to the compilers of the ancient manuscript of Wyrd, love is an energy that we can attract into our lives. The way to find love is not to go out looking for it, but to know how to feel it in one's own life, to draw on its sustenance, to weave it into our very being.

The secret to bringing it into your life is to know how much you are loved. And once we know that, in our heart, love comes to us in every way. And it simply grows in our hearts to fill us with warmth, happiness, health and wealth.

Golden Threads of Love

The wizards of old saw us as being suspended in the centre of our own web of golden threads of love. The threads suspend, connect and integrate everything in our life. The threads are so sensitive that any thought, any emotion, any event, no matter how small, reverberates throughout the entire web. This is indeed how scientists see life today. It was very like our contemporary physics, but wrought with beautiful images. It shows us how to attune to all aspects of our lives, and it is the key to our feelings of love.

CREATE YOUR OWN WEB

Try this creative, practical and powerful meditation on how much you are loved.

Take a sheet of paper, and a pen.

List the names of everyone you know with whom you have a positive relationship. But do it only from memory. Don't consult your address book or email files. Just list those people you can think of. It should take no more than an hour to write down all the appropriate names. But take your time.

Next take a large sheet of paper and draw a map of the world. Or at least the country where you live. Copy it from an atlas. It doesn't have to be exact, so long as it gives a reasonable sense of the geographical extent and location of those parts of the world you are going to incorporate in your Wyrd meditation.

Mark with a dot the place on the map where you currently live. Then mark on the map the locations of each of the people named on your list. Again, take your time. Treat it like a meditation.

You'll end up with a map with some names dotted far and wide, and a greater number being marked nearer to your own home location. But everyone's map is different, there are no 'right' or 'wrong' maps.

The final stage is to carefully draw straight lines leading from the dot representing your own location to every other dot on the map. Be as creative and colourful as you like.

The map now looks like a huge spider's web, and we can see our position in it. Many I have worked with on such webs are often surprised to see all those threads coming into them from around the country, or around the world.

It shows the threads of positive energy that come your way from people who mean a lot to you.

Use the map as a meditation on how much you are loved. Seeing it as a whole, as an image, rather than as separate names in our address book, changes our feelings about how we are loved. If you are feeling low, discouraged or lonely, this simple meditation can be very supportive.

Knowing how much we are loved changes our presence in the world. It alters how we think of ourselves, how we are in relationships. It makes us more confident, more generous, more loving toward others. It is like a magnet, it draws love into your life. To know how much you are loved is the single most important thing you can do to draw love into your life. It is a wonderful secret from the ancient wizards of Wyrd.

• •

Kelfin Oberon

Here's my newest and very personal poem about how babies save the world by the very nature of love.

A Little Bird Told Me No Worries

Borne on the wing of a prayer
As two ships passed in one night
Spirit in the wind guided our sails
Sheltering the sudden stirring storm
Spirit brought both our boats to birth
In the same bay
On the same day

Relation ships stick together and drift apart
Drift together and get blown a part

A beautiful baby beams in to birth
A shining star soul breathes new life into Earth

Star Trek trajectory
Gaia's dream gene factory
Star Date Log 20 13
12 separate di visions become one dream
12 separate tribes join one DNA stream
All types of every thing
All in one gene

My kids have a mix of their mothers and me
A genetic mutation of a new generation
Born into a world more conscious and free

We face salvation or total annihilation
So it's simple to see what the answer will be

It's well worth knowing that life is all ways growing
Ever lasting miracle of eternity.

Chris Fleming

Always remember there is no greater love, no greater joy than the smile on another's face and the look in their eyes when you have helped them or given them your love.

● ●

John Briffa

I don't want to make out that my life is an endless bowl of cherries, but I do at least feel quite blessed to be doing work I am truly passionate about, and also gain considerable strength and comfort from feeling loved and supported by both family and friends.

However, one area I have historically found to be persistently problematic is that of romantic relationships. To be frank, while I have generally found getting into relationships relatively easily, my experience has also been that getting out of them has been even easier. After the initial rush of excitement that can come with the birth of a new union, I have often found myself shutting off emotionally from my partner. This detachment would usually come in the matter of a few short months and often, it seemed, for little good reason.

I suppose, like a lot of mere mortals, I have had a tendency in the past to believe that my relationship 'problems' were rooted in compatibility issues stemming from my partners' inability to give me what I wanted or needed. However, in recent years, it occurred to me that one consistent factor in all my relationships was me! Could it be that something deep in my psyche might be causing me to repeat a pattern that was not only of my making, but that only I could change?

Lianne, a close friend of mine, suggested that my relationship issues might stem from events in my past, possibly as far back as my very first experiences of life. Intuitively, this made sense to me: I knew my gestation and birth had been fraught with difficulty.

While in the womb, a fundamental incompatibility between mine and my mother's blood meant that her immune cells systematically broke down my red blood cells, leaving me profoundly anaemic. So badly affected was I by this process that even prior to being born I twice required additional blood which was given via a needle inserted through my mother's womb and into my own body under X-ray control.

My birth was induced more than a month early, and I was so critically ill after being born that I had to be immediately removed from my mother for emergency care. Over the next two days, the blood in my body was completely exchanged for that from a donor no less than three times. Only after 10 days of intensive medical treatment and monitoring was I allowed home.

I am eternally grateful to my parents for giving me life, and to the medical staff who cared for me and my mother around the time of my birth. In many senses, I know how very lucky I am to be alive. However, at the same time, it seemed to me that my friend's suggestion that such a troubled start to my existence might in some way have affected my experiences in later life was far from far-fetched. In particular, it seemed reasonable to me that my early relationship with my mother, though no fault of hers, was one mainly coloured by rejection and separation, and that this might somehow have led to the relationship issues I was keen to resolve.

While deep-set emotional and psychological issues may be approached in myriad ways, it seemed appropriate that my particular issues might be best resolved through the practice of 'rebirthing'. Typical rebirthing sessions incorporate a discussion which is followed by the therapist supporting the client through a breathing process which is designed to facilitate the release of undesirable thoughts and emotions. Not without trepidation, I embarked on a series of sessions with a practitioner by the name of Pat Bennaceur.

In my first session, Pat explored with me the life issues I felt I was having, along with the circumstances of my gestation and birth. I got to explore much more deeply than I ever had before what were likely to have been my early emotions. My 'remembering' of this time left me feeling bereft of any sense of intimacy. In subsequent sessions, other intense emotions that I experienced also included fear of loss, insecurity and a need to protect myself. I make no secret of the fact that sessions would usually be powerful and challenging, and often moved me to tears. However, after each session, I would always feel that I had a much greater understanding of myself, coupled with a very real sense that something had been released. Through Pat's love, support and expertise, I felt I was able to integrate and transform emotions that appeared to be holding me back from having a truly fulfilled relationship.

Some months after this process started, I embarked on my current relationship. From the beginning, I was honest with Karen about the relationship issues I had traditionally been challenged with, and the fact that I was attempting to resolve these through the practice of rebirthing. Karen was very loving and supportive in regard to this, and I felt a tremendous amount of relief from simply 'getting things out into the open'. And, while old patterns recur from time to time and I do still have the capacity to retreat within myself, one major difference is that I am much more conscious of my feelings and actions, where they come from, and what to do about them. I sense a new openness within myself, which I think has enriched my relationship not just with Karen, but others too. A by-product of the rebirthing process was that I talked to my parents about the circumstances of my birth for the first time in almost 40 years – something that I believe has helped to bring us closer.

The importance of my recent experiences was brought into sharp focus soon after I met Karen. The first time I came to her home I realized that she lived literally next door to the hospital in which I was born, in a part of London I had never revisited since my birth. It was like the Universe was confirming to me how important reconciling my birth experience was to my ability to have the sort of relationship I had always longed for.

●●

Sonia Choquette

Q *Sun sign and other planetary influences*

A Libra sun, Libra rising, Aries moon, five planets in Libra and the twelfth house.

Q *Favourite thing about what you do*

A I love people and I love finding solutions to people's problems. My philosophy is, 'There is always a solution, no matter how challenging the situation.' I love the complexity of the human soul, and find the evolution of the soul the most fascinating subject in the world. I never get tired of it. I am constantly amazed by the creativity behind all soul dramas and love to show people how their souls are setting up their life paths for growth. Once a person understands that everything that happens to them – *everything* – is for their soul's growth, life becomes fascinating, manageable and exciting. Drama gives way to creativity and obstacles become opportunities.

Q *Secret way of pampering or healing yourself that makes you feel amazing*

A I renew myself by travelling with my husband and kids to exotic places where no one knows me and I do not focus on anyone else's troubles. On these trips we have a shared adventure as a family and we laugh a lot. We prefer places that offer excitement. We take at least one trip a year. Last year we went to India. This year we are going to Argentina. These trips feed the well of my spirit and give me lots of creative juices.

I also love music and dancing and am secretly a musician at heart. I sing rock-and-roll songs at the op of my lungs while driving along in my bright blue VW bug all over town.

Q *Favourite place in the world?*

A My favorite place in the world is Egypt. I got engaged there at the foot of the Great Pyramid at dawn 23 years ago. I have returned with my husband and children several times and love it all the more each time I go. I equally love India. I believe my soul is from India and I draw from many past lives there.

Q *Secret fantasy to make the world a better place*

A To get everyone singing and dancing and 'over themselves' and into their spirit.

Q *Future secrets – what do you know about where we're heading?*

A I see several serious new sources of energy developing and a significant shift away from dependency on fossil fuels, which will shift the balance of power. There has been exciting news from Japan in this regard.

I feel the purge of old energies will continue for three more years (up to 2008/9), which will result in many more international disasters. The more we personally release and renew stagnant behaviours and judgement of others, and commit to living a higher way, the less severe these changes will be.

There are cures for diabetes and Alzheimer's on the horizon as well.

We are heading to a more conscious awareness of our dependency on one another and the futility of trying to separate ourselves in factions.

I believe the best thing you can do for this planet and your own soul at this time is to choose to be happy and peaceful in your own heart, and to love yourself. It is a dynamic choice and one that takes a great deal of resolution and courage as this world does not necessarily value or encourage those choices. By listening to your spirit, your sixth sense, you can begin to feel happy and peaceful, and deeply love yourself. Without your sixth sense it is not possible.

Perry Wood

Ultimately everything is love; there is an infinite supply of love and anything that expresses itself to the contrary is based on fear ... which can be healed and removed with love. Simple (but maybe not always easy!)!

I believe we all have what we might call angels taking care of us, and that we are never alone, they are always listening and always helping.

I have recently sent unconditional love silently to a couple of people I have had difficulty with, and without changing anything else, and without their being consciously aware of it, it has transformed my relationships with them overnight. The power of love never ceases to amaze.

• •

Dadi Janki

Q *What is your favourite activity?*

A Staying in the awareness of and experiencing the true qualities of the soul: love, peace and happiness. Connecting with the Supreme Soul in meditation and taking enough strength and power to be an instrument to spread vibrations of peace around a troubled world.

Q *How do you meditate and relax completely?*

A I practice Raja Yoga meditation, which is very simple to do. We meditate with our eyes open, in a relaxed sitting position, and focus on a point in the centre of our foreheads. Gently concentrating on this point, I use my thought power to connect with my inner being. In just a few seconds, I am able to experience the quality of pure inner peace that is my foundation. In silence, and in stillness, I detach my thoughts from the outside world and spend time experiencing the non-material, subtle form of the soul.

This body is just an instrument through which I can express myself. The soul is the eternal, living being that performs through the body. By immersing my thoughts in the qualities of the soul I am able to feel calm, to create a space for silence. We can only relax completely when we have removed all negative thinking from our minds. When we use every breath in a worthwhile way, there is no room for waste. When there is no waste, then I have no worries.

In the stillness created through the awareness of the peaceful being that I am, I connect with the Divine: the Being of Light, the Source of Love.

Q *Is there anywhere in the world where you can feel very peaceful?*

A I can feel peaceful in any situation, but there is a place that has special meaning for me. It is in Mount Abu in Rajasthan. There is a special promontory called Baba's Rock very close to the village. I was in my early twenties when I first went there, with other founding members of the Brahma Kumaris World Spiritual University (BKWSU). It's about twenty minutes' walk from the BKWSU headquarters. We used to climb up to the rock every evening and meditate until sunset. High up in the mountains overlooking a plain, when you meditate you really feel that you have flown out of this world. After nearly 70 years of groups of meditators heading up to Baba's

Rock to enjoy this special experience, you can feel a special spiritual energy there.

Q *Do you have a secret wish that would make the world a better place?*

A I don't think my wishes are very secret. It is a fact that I support and encourage a healthy spiritual lifestyle for everyone. I share my experience of being a soul with everyone I come into contact with. It is only when we remove ourselves from the focus on material things to an understanding of our true being that we will make the world a better place. The quality that we most need to develop for this is peace. When I build up my stocks of inner peace, then I will be in a position to create a more harmonious world with every step I take.

Q *As a Keeper of Wisdom, do you have any insights into what the future holds for us?*

A Not on the level of predicting the future, but on the understanding of cycles of time. We are in a period of intense transformation at all levels and, in a way, the world is trying to rid itself of toxins and pollution.

There are many individuals and communities around the world working for a more positive and healthy environment, where distribution of the world's resources is more balanced.

I see that we are in a transition period that will eventually lead to a world of peace, harmony and balance, where we all have respect for each other and a vision of the soul in our interactions.

As human souls change and return to their original divine state, the world around us changes to one of truth, love and justice. The present and immediate future is one of chaos and much upheaval. The connection with the Divine brings purity and stability with which we can create the foundation of a better world beyond the chaos.

Wayne Dyer

On Love and Optimism

Optimism is knowing that you create what is your intention. I'm always very optimistic. I think being pessimistic makes you one of the people that are part of the problem and it never resolves anything.

I don't want to be full of hatred towards people who are displaying hate themselves. People participating in war and those who hate war are on the same pathway. Going around all day feeling hate and living in fear is not going to change what's already happened. And when everyone is fearful, we just create more of the very thing that we are most afraid of.

You have to be able to send love. With the war in Iraq

and the problems in the Middle East, you surround everyone involved with love and say, 'I didn't sign up for this. This is not a part of my consciousness.' Trust that ultimately they'll get to a place where they'll find peace. By being loving and feeling optimistic, even in the face of what's going on around you, you change the energy field and have a much better chance of shifting what's going on in the world.

Martin Luther King Jnr said that the only way to convert an enemy into a friend is through love. You can never do it through violence. Because if I start killing your family in order to make you into a democracy, I just create more families who, 20 years later, are filled with hatred for what I did.

We need to sit down and talk about why all these people in the world hate the West so much. We don't have to agree with them. Let's just find out what it is that we're doing in the West that they find so offensive and see how we can come to a meeting place. That's what you do in a family when you've got people who are angry and bitter. You don't just keep throwing things at each other, becoming more furious.

There's too much attention placed on what is wrong in our society. Albert Einstein said that the most important decision you'll ever make is whether you live in a friend-ly universe or a hostile one. Because when you change the way you look at things, the things you look at change. That's not just a fancy way with words; that's a quantum truth. On a quantum physics level, when you observe a sub-atomic particle, the way you observe it determines how it behaves. Change the way you observe the world and you literally change the world you're observing.

Yet, we get inundated with constant bad news, so we believe that's the nature of things. But it's not. Man's basic instinct is to be kind. After Hurricane Katrina, in 2005, more money was collected than has ever been collected in the history of the United States. Congress was barely able to muster up $10 billion, despite the fact that it happened in three states, large areas, and thousands of people were displaced. Perversely, when we decided to go to war in Iraq, in two years they raised $400 billion. Wouldn't it be interesting if we could reverse that?

Ultimately, I believe we live in a friendly universe and for every act of horror and hate, there are a million acts of kindness. I think more and more people are believing the same. My hope is that there'll be enough high spiritual, strengthening energy to compensate for the numbers of people who live in ego consciousness and think that we can kill our way to peace. What the outcome will be we can only speculate. But I have a knowing within that good will triumph.

I find inspiration everywhere. To be inspired means to be in spirit, and to be in spirit means to be connected to the Source. My mother inspires me. She worked hard to get her family back together again in the face of phenomenal odds during the Depression and then the war. Gandhi inspires me. Mother Teresa inspires me. Bees, ants, birds, butterflies. A Boeing 747. Air. Fire inspires the hell out of me; what is it exactly and where does it come from? And the same goes for water, which makes up 65 percent of the human body. It's incredible.

Virtually every person I meet inspires me. I walk through the streets and think we're all connected and we're all here because loving is so good. Imagine if loving each other and having sex felt bad! Everybody is here because people want to love each other and be close to one another. So we all got here in the same way. We're all part of this great big love fest and we just don't know it.

SENSUAL, SEXUAL SECRETS

Silja

To feel more sensual and to encourage loving energies between you and your partner, have him massage you with almond oil, and make sure he rubs it in a clockwise motion. Once he's finished with your back, he can always move on to other places …

Barefoot Doctor

Providing there's a chemistry between you and someone, and the circumstances vaguely permit, if you stroke extremely lightly along the crease on the inside of the elbow joint from outside to inside (with their arm bent and palm facing upwards), 18 times, ending with the inward stroke, you will be making love with them within three hours.

Laura Berridge

Take time to include all the senses, to feel really alive and 'in' your body – play music to echo your desired mood, lovingly massage the face and body with fragrant lotions (rose and vanilla are favourites) and layer with complementary perfumes. I wear colours and clothes to adorn my inner Goddess, reflect my mood and skim my body with sensual textures. Finally, I have a meditation to open all the chakras softly, in which I see myself entering a beautiful garden ... and then becoming the garden ... and the party in the garden ...

• •

Chuck Spezzano

I believe I can do more to help the world get over its sexual repression and corresponding kinkiness in my present work. My bawdy, outrageous humour seems to fit this task perfectly. The humour of relationships and sex is never-ending. I believe one of the promises I made when I came into this life was to help bring naturalness back to human beings.

Sex and the body are both illusions in a world of dreams, but too many people are imprisoned in sexual shame, guilt and karma. As The Foundation for Inner Peace's *A Course in Miracles* reminds us: 'This need not be.' So I believe we must untangle the greater illusion of sexual pain and judgement before we can release the illusions of sex and the body for the joy of soul communion.

It looks like we have millions and millions of years left to heal sexual pain, so we can transcend it all as beings of light. Until then, there's a lot to laugh about and heal, and when we succeed, there are love, respect and slippery celebrations!

· ·

Leora Lightwoman

My approach to Tantra

Tantra is a path of spiritual and sexual ecstasy. Ecstasy means going beyond the ordinary, beyond your normal frame of reference. And yet I see Tantra fundamentally as a path of recognizing more deeply and compassionately our essential humanity. It's a wonderful paradox. Ecstatic sex and ecstatic living happen when life is lived fully in the Now. And in the Now we meet ourselves, our limitations, our beliefs, our feelings, our vulnerability.

Often there are aspects of ourselves that we want to change. And yet the more willing that we are simply to feel and accept our experience in the moment, the more swiftly that feeling will move on, and sooner or later the natural joy, bliss and passion of our Being will come through. We don't have to go searching for ecstasy, only to recognize it in small things and to let go of constantly striving for it and getting in its way.

Young children have a lot to show us. They are natural, spontaneous, vulnerable, excitable and they know how to play, laugh and have fun. If, as adults, we can live in a way that is infused with these qualities, life and sex will naturally have a sparkle. When your daily life and inner experience are sensual, sexy, scintillating and sweet, you don't have to go looking for the biggest and best orgasms or most gorgeous partner to do it for you. You become more content and intimate.

I myself was first attracted to Tantra because I wanted better orgasms. I thought they would bring me more fulfilment and intimacy. I ended up finding fulfilment, intimacy and self-responsibility first, and orgasms later. I discovered that when I'm open and available, then the Universe, the Great Mystery, has space to move in, and bliss and true union can happen.

Alicen Geddes-Ward

This is my secret, you fill in the gaps …

Through following faeriecraft I have learnt that sex does not have to be just a physical encounter, but it can also be experienced astrally too. In the year 2000 I had one of the most profound visitation dream experiences I have ever had, where I was given the parting words, 'Sex is a spiritual art.' Walking the path of the faerie is to be sexually free, where you can experience freedom of the inner spirit and you connect to the light.

Faerie Land is a place of magical sexual allurement, where faeries are the spiritual embodiments of nature, the sexiest thing on Earth. Nature is sex, part of the ingredients of the magical spark of life. Connecting to that creative energy does not have to be a physical encounter, it can also be one of the imagination leading to astral experiences whether you are actively conscious of them or involuntarily encounter them in the dream realm. Sex is a meeting of two worlds and sometimes can be a way to enter Faerie Land to meld with another to experience a blissful part of the divine.

- -

Adam Fronteras

Your dreams can often show your sexual wishes. Sometimes it's a way of allowing our mind to go through things and situations that we would find uncomfortable in real life. Dreams of a sensual nature should not be feared and even if weird they do not always mean that we long for that experience; a dream is a safe environment in which to have that experience.

- -

Kate West

I don't feel that sensuality and sexuality are inextricably linked. Many of the most sensual things in life have little or nothing to do with sexuality: the scent of freshly baked bread, a cat rubbing around my bare legs, the feel of spring rain on my skin, the flavour of freshly cooked prawns eaten whilst sitting watching the sea. I love a really big thunderstorm to make me feel exhilarated and full of energy again.

In the absence of a storm (after all, it wouldn't be fair to go around summoning them just because I feel like it) then a lovely deep candlelit bath with aromatherapy oils and bubbles, followed by sitting in front of a real fire sipping some wine and nibbling at small squares of really dark chocolate.

SPELLS & SIGNS, CHARMS & CHANTS

Silja

I love it when previously sceptical people get excited about a spell working.

Back in college, a friend of mine who was a postgrad had difficulty with the other postgrad she was sharing an office with. The other student kept making fun of her research and putting her work down in front of her supervisor, and it started to affect my friend's confidence.

I offered to help her with a spell, but she said she wasn't a witch and didn't know how to do one, and so it wouldn't work. I explained that while being experienced helps, complete beginners can make simple spells work.

I suggested she put five red pencils into a pentagram shape, with one point pointing towards the other postgrad, to neutralize that person's negative energy. A week later, the other postgrad got a lot of typing work from their supervisor and was kept too busy to harass my friend!

Another time, a new member of the coven gave me a lift into town as we were going to the theatre. But it was Friday evening and we couldn't find a parking space anywhere. So, I took a piece of chocolate out of my bag and, holding in in front of the rearview mirror, chanted:

'Parking fairy give to us
a parking space as big as a bus.
Chocolate I have for you,
your help to us you will not rue!'

The new coven member laughed as she watched me wave the chocolate in front of the mirror, but she quickly shut up when she saw, in her rearview mirror, a car pull out of the ideal parking spot, just 20 yards from the theatre entrance!

I started my witchy career with tarot reading and meditations, and I guess the first truly magical thing I did was a money spell, because I was a poor student and wanted to attend a concert.

I lit a green candle and asked for money to come to me, but no ill to be done to anyone (you have to be careful with money spells, so that you don't get the money because of an accident and you getting compensation, or a loved one dying and leaving you money). I did find £5 on the ground the next day, but it wasn't enough for the concert ticket.

Believe it or not, I rarely do spells for myself. I see them as a last resort after having done everything you can in the mundane world.

But there are some magical techniques and ingredients that I use often.

The most popular visualisation, versions of which I often recommend, is to imagine a bubble of blue, healing light around a person who is sick or is in need of protection.

Ingredients that I often use are nutmeg for luck, amber to foster good relationships, rose quartz for love and basil leaves to draw money to you.

For luck and success:

Add three tablespoons of ground nutmeg to a warm bath and immerse yourself fully three times after saying:

'Change of luck come to be / as I will it, so mote it be!'

To draw success in business or financial matters to you, carry five almonds, ideally still in their shell.

Most successful spell ever:

For me: keeping a copper penny covered in green wax in my wallet, to ensure I always have money – it worked even when I was unemployed for more than six months.

Going by readers' feedback: to bring two people together if they are truly meant to be together, or strengthen a relationship which has grown apart – place two pink candles (use yellow candles if this is a friendship rather than love relationship) about a yard apart on a mantelpiece. Each day, light the candles for 10 minutes or more, while thinking about how happy you will be together, and what you are going to do to help the relationship. Blow out the candles, and move each about an inch closer together; repeat each day until the candles touch, then let the candles burn down fully.

● ●

Carina Coen

Lucky charm: My beautiful sweet fluffy unicorn mini handbag definitely brings me luck. Plus, it always makes others smile and has women wondering if it's a designer handbag.

Ritual: Bathtime with my merfolk and faeries, of course!

Mantra for good luck:

> *Yesterday is history*
> *Tomorrow is a a mystery*
> *Today is a gift, so ENJOY!*

● ●

Sonia Choquette

I use several mantras for support –

'OM Mane Padme OM' for healing, expansion and blessings.

'Elohim' for abundance and manifestation.

I use the Egyptian mantra, *'Su HETP NA!'* to cut cords and release myself from negative energies.

And every day I say, *'I lead a charmed life'*, to anyone who asks how I am.

It comes true.

●●●

Cassandra Eason

I only live five minutes from the sea. Before I go away, I always go out down to the water's edge and get a little bit of water in a screw-top glass bottle and say, 'Keep me safe till I return.'

I then tuck the bottle under the roots of my favourite lavender bush in my garden. When I come back I go down to the sea, tip the water back in and say, 'I return what is yours. Thank you for keeping me safe.'

HOME SECRETS

....

Summer Watson

The Spirit of Place

Wherever you are, whatever you are doing, you are in a magical relationship with the land beneath you. It doesn't matter whether you are relaxing at home, having a busy day at the office or meditating on top of a mountain, you are being affected by the energies in the Earth there and they are being affected by you. Human beings have always had this exquisite dance with the spirit of place and there is a deep joy in learning how to tune into this – especially in your home.

Our Earth is a living being criss-crossed by energy lines, in much the same way that we have meridians in our bodies. Sometimes known as Ley Lines, they flow like rivers carrying currents of energy that affect our health, our life-path, our luck and our very soul. Your life can be changed dramatically by the energies that flow through your home but, once you can 'read' them, you can work with them in a positive way. By looking at the shape of your house, the direction it faces, its history, as well as dowsing for the energies beneath it, you can start to reveal its true personality and develop a relationship with it that supports you. I believe it is no accident that we are drawn to the houses that we live in – they choose us as much as we choose them!

In my work I have come across properties with all sorts of personalities: wealth houses, poverty houses, houses that support relationships and houses that don't, creative houses, sick houses, lucky houses, jinxed houses and haunted houses. To enrich your life and your soul, I encourage you to get to know your home in this way, become good friends with it and maybe find out why destiny has brought the two of you together.

Gina Lazenby

I have always felt that our homes are reflections of who we are – I point this out to clients and get them to reflect on how the environment of their home might be a mirror for what is going on in their life. My experience of this in my own home has been profound and enlightening. As I now live in two homes – one in the Yorkshire Dales and the other in London, I have really had the opportunity to road-test this idea.

When the boiler breaks down in one house it will usually break down in the other around the same time. When the washing machine broke in Yorkshire, sure enough the washer stopped in London too. When the water was mysteriously cut off one night in London, within an hour the Yorkshire water pump also stopped! When there was an attempted burglary of the London property I was immediately concerned for my Yorkshire home, particularly as I was preparing to leave for a week away. Although the Yorkshire house remained secure, when I returned I found we had been broken into, but not by humans – by sheep. A flock had invaded our garden and devastated most of the shrubs!

Each time these events happen in duplicate I have to ask myself what this means and what I can learn from the experience. Invariably when I am forced to stop and pay attention to what is going on around me, my reflection and meditation will lead me to some necessary change in my way of being that sets me on the right track again and the house goes back to normal. It's very interesting viewing your home as a teacher.

. . . .

Cassandra Eason

Most treasured possession is my clear quartz crystal ball. It's full of cracks, having been carried on my travels and bounced by various children. I use it in so many ways – set in impersonal hotel rooms as a centre and a piece of home, as a healing tool filled with sunlight and moonlight, and reading the pictures inside as a form of guidance when the way is not clear for myself or others. I also use my crystal ball to talk to my overworked guardian angel, an older woman angel who finds it hard to get my attention as I race through life. As I make contact, with my palms round the sphere, it brings together all the jangling aspects of my psyche, calms my jittery nerves before a major talk or broadcast and centres me when I'm far from home.

Sarah Shurety

In Chinese astrology I'm a metal rat. We are charming, survivors, open and loyal. Rats tend to be leaders who have a gift of communication and are constantly on the move. But we can also be impatient, and not very good at keeping secrets.

My grandmother taught me there's no such word as 'can't'.

I do not value any possessions highly. The Feng Shui concept is that we come into this life with nothing and we go out with nothing and we should never put a high value on objects. My most treasured possession is the love and support I share with my family, my partner and his beautiful daughter, my friends and the animals in my life.

For good luck, I always use my special green Feng Shui purse with a set of I Ching coins in it, which help me to keep a balance between money, health and love.

I love exploring a new self-development course or alternative healing process like macrobiotics, acupuncture, Chinese herbs, Ayurvedic medicine, NLP, going to an ashram or though a detoxification and regeneration session.

Having a picnic and watching the sunset with my best friend and partner Mike Yuille is my idea of perfect happiness.

You have to work at relationships as the world is in the middle cycle of single living, according to Feng Shui. This means that it's more difficult to stay in a close, tolerant and happy relationship with our partners and families. Mike and I have a photograph of each other – looking into each other's eyes or kissing – in practically every room in our house and we have lots of artworks of couples who appear genuinely in love. This helps to re-inforce our love. It's also important not to spread 'poison' by complaining about loved ones.

• •

Louise L. Hay

Blessing Your Work

Maybe you are in a job right now that you don't like and just going through the motions for the money, or you feel bored and stuck in a rut. Well, there are definitely positive things that that you could do to change things. These ideas may sound silly or too simple, but I know that they work. I have seen countless numbers of people radically improve the quality of their working day.

The most powerful tool that I can share with you to transform a situation is the power of *blessing with love*. No matter where you work or how you feel about the place, *bless it with love*. I mean this literally, don't just try and think generally positive thoughts in a vague way; instead, say, 'I bless this job with love.' Find somewhere that you can say this out loud: there is so much power in giving voice to love.

Don't stop there. Bless everything in your workplace with love: the equipment, the furniture, the machines, the products, the customers, the people you work with and the people you work for, and anything else associated with your job. It will work wonders.

It might be that you have personal difficulties with someone at your work. If so, use your mind to change the situation. Affirmations work incredibly well for this. Say, '*I have a wonderful relationship with everyone at work, including* ___.' Every time that person comes into your mind repeat the affirmation. You will be amazed at how the relationship improves. A solution may come about that you cannot even imagine at the moment. Just speak the words and let the Universe sort out the details.

If you are thinking about getting a new job, then in addition to blessing your current job add the affirmation: 'I release this job to the next person, who will be so glad to be here.' That particular job was ideal for you at the time you got it. Now your sense of self-worth has grown and you are ready to move on to better things. Your affirmation now is: 'I know there are people out there who are looking for exactly what I have to offer. I now accept a job that uses all my creative talents and abilities. This job is deeply fulfilling, and it is a joy for me to go to work each day. I work for people who appreciate me. The building is light, bright and airy and filled with a feeling of enthusiasm. It is in the perfect location and I earn good money, for which I am deeply grateful.'

If you hate the job that you have now, there is a danger that you will take that hatred with you when you move to a new job. However good the new job is, you will soon find yourself hating that job too. Whatever feelings or thoughts you have within you now will be carried to the new place. If you live within a world of discontentment you will find it wherever you go. Only by changing your consciousness now will you start to see positive results in your life. If you do this, then when the new job comes along it will be good and you will be able to really enjoy it.

So if you currently hate your job try the affirmation: 'I always love where I work. I have the best jobs. I am always appreciated.' By continually affirming this you are creating a new personal law for yourself, and the Universe will respond in kind. Like attracts like and Life will always look for routes of bringing good towards you, if you allow it.

EARTH SECRETS

....

Jon Sandifer

The most powerful way to make me feel at one with the world and universe is to sleep out under the stars. I spent six years travelling the world from the ages of 17 to 23, and have lost count of how many nights I slept under the stars. It's the most invigorating experience. I have been fortunate enough to sleep out in the most exciting places, such as the Sahara, Afghanistan, Kilimanjaro, beaches in Indonesia and Malaysia, and the Seychelles. But even a flat rooftop in an urban environment can provide much the same buzz.

The best setting for meditation is obviously somewhere peaceful. I learnt this the hard way when I was 17 and living in a cave in Formentera, Spain, after I had run away from school. Early in the morning I used to see this French hippy guy appear and wander along to a very tall, jagged pillar of rock, situated some 30 feet above the water line. I'd watch in admiration as he clambered up to the top and then, sitting in his sarong in a lotus position, he would face out toward the sunrise. Wow! I thought that was something to learn. Having observed him for a few mornings, I decided to try this myself. However, I chose a particularly stormy morning for my first venture. I scrambled up to the top with just a towel tied round my waist, sat like he had been sitting, facing the same direction, and had no idea what to expect. Massive waves were pounding against the pillar, which sent showers of spray over my head. It was exhilarating and I thought, if this is meditation, I can do more of this. However, the third wave knocked me right off the top and I was sent down the side of the pillar and received several cuts; some of them to this day remain scars. The lesson I learnt was to find a peaceful spot to meditate, but also somewhere safe and secure!

Penney Poyzer

Q *Most treasured possession and why?*

A My classical guitar, which I have had since I was five. I have very few possesions from my early life, so this is pretty special. I still play, and the tone of the guitar is mellow and wonderful.

Q *Secret eco-friendly way of pampering and/or healing yourself that makes you feel amazing*

A Living in my ecohome is very healing. From chopping wood for the boiler to heat the house, to knowing that there are no toxins present in my home, to preparing food from our weekly organic box – it all makes me feel good. The quality of my life is amazing and I am very grateful for it.

Q *Diet and exercise tips which really work – and have least impact on the planet*

A Our diet contains no processed food at all; it is all cooked from fresh and is 90% organic. I love my bicycle, it is practical and a great way to get around. The saddle is built like a sofa, so my bum loves it too!

Q *Most profound, life-changing dream*

A When I was about 18, I had the most awful repeating dream about nuclear war. In the dream, the birds stopped singing and a child's bicycle lay abandoned in the middle of the street, the back wheel slowly turning. I was overwhelmed by a sense of grief over the loss of all forms of life through pointless war. Once I got over the image (which I can still recall as if it were yesterday), I vowed to put as much positive energy into the planet as I could. It remains my mantra.

Q *Deep beliefs that keep you going when things are tough*

A I put my trust in the Universe and turn to it for an extra boost of energy when my resources are low.

Q *Who or what inspires you most and why?*

A Gandhi is my abiding inspiration. That one person could achieve so much, through peaceable means, shows that the power of their spirit and the love of mankind is the greatest example of how the human spirit can achieve a higher state and be a profound source of goodness.

Q *Secret fantasy to make the world a better place*

A Get rid of Blair and Bush for a start, and get leaders with vision and conscience.

Q *Future secrets – what do you know about where we're heading?*

A I believe that problems with global clean water supplies and rises in sea levels will be hitting us much sooner than we imagined. Within the next five years we will see huge numbers of deaths from thirst and lack of food because of low rainfall. I believe that next summer the UK will see water-rationing. Within five years we will see much more flooding on our coastal regions and more flooding in Europe and China.

• •

Jude Currivan

Message to self ...

Although the manifestation of crop circles goes back centuries, it is only in the last few decades that the arrival of intricate formations has resulted in reactions ranging from wonder to disdain.

Whilst becoming a worldwide phenomenon, its heartland is within the landscape of southwest England, especially the rolling chalkland – the white land – around Avebury.

Here, the formations of these 'temporary temples' that often embody geometric harmony, resonate powerfully with this sacred land and the monuments that date back to the Neolithic era of up to six millennia ago.

Research suggests that their formation involves vortices of electro-magnetic fields and sonic energies. Whilst the affected plants of these living mandalas remain unharmed, the subsequent growth patterns from their seeds show significant differences from those of seeds from unaffected plants in the same field.

But answers to the questions of why they are created and who the circle makers are remain enigmatic. And despite the claims of so-called hoaxers, the accumulated evidence does not support human agency as being their sole and easily dismissable cause.

Rather than taking a role in the often contentious debate surrounding them, I have chosen personally to focus on their message rather than on the identity of the messenger or indeed how the message is delivered.

* * * *

My initiation into their message began in early 1995, when I was 43, and was so empowering that within a few months I had moved home to live in the heart of the Avebury landscape.

In the beginning, my quest was to understand the phenomenon. But, as I allowed myself to let go of my innate need to comprehend its details, I began to experience its deeper magic. By being open to the lessons I was being offered, I was repeatedly gifted with intuitive insights and a sense of being nurtured by Gaia, the living

Earth. Like many others, I began to appreciate its benevolence as a harbinger of change, if we are willing to listen. On a personal level, it guided me along a path of inner healing and helped me to further sensitize myself to subtle energies and the quiet voice of Spirit.

I soon found that I was able to commune with the devic and elemental beings within the landscape and the aetheric guardians of the ancient sites. A wonderland of heart-based wisdom was now open to me, whose depths I continue to explore and for which I am ever grateful.

* * * *

One particular crop circle became the seed-point of further revelations – when on a gentle afternoon in May 1998, my higher guidance offered the seemingly innocuous message to 'go to Silbury Hill tomorrow'.

The next morning, approaching this energetic nexus of the Avebury landscape, I saw a formation in the oil-seed rape to the south of the hill, from whose summit its full glory was revealed – a golden disc nearly 200 feet across.

As I attuned to its energies, I felt a deep sense of peace as though all my questions had been answered, but I didn't understand what those questions had been!

The seed of that experience gestated for nine months, during which time the life I had known fell away – my marriage broke up, I lost my home and my work-life

collapsed. But by its completion, I was ready to undertake the first steps of an outer journey that was to take me
around the world – and an inner journey beyond imagining.

* * * *

My higher guidance told me that the disc-like glyph of
the crop circle reflected an aetheric Disc located beneath
Silbury Hill. What's more, that it was one of 12 located
around the world, the activation of whose healing
energies would support individual and collective shifts of
awareness.

These Discs are multi-dimensional but primarily exist in
higher spiritual or aetheric form. They are interconnect-
ed with the aetheric grid of the Earth, the consciousness
of our individual and collective soul purpose, the entire
solar – or 'soul-ar' – system, and the galaxy. The Discs
were gifted to the Lemurian people 39,000 years ago by
the Elohim – the spiritual guides of the evolution of our
entire solar system.

It may sound like science fiction, but such Discs and the
aetheric grid of the Earth have been known to
geomancers through the millennia. The Earth's dodeca-
hedral grid was first mentioned by Plato two-and-a-half
thousand years ago. And in the 1970s, three Soviet
researchers announced a grid of Earth energies which
corresponded to ancient understanding, and that in

physical terms equates to electro-magnetic stress lines around the globe.

* * * *

Eventually, I was guided to offer an odyssey of 12 sacred journeys around the world to activate the Discs. Together they formed a three-year pilgrimage, to 12 countries, with nearly 70 other spiritual souls from all walks of life and location, ranging in age from a young man in his teens to several people in their late seventies. The journeys' purpose of global transformation ultimately became a revelation of our human and planetary destiny.

As we journeyed, more intense information flowed and we experienced wave after wave of synchronicities and validations, which were crucial to us all to make sense of everything.

These 12 pilgrimages were to be completed by early November 2003 and, enigmatically, a '13th master key' was to be turned at Avebury on 23rd December 2003.

As the journeys progressed, to Egypt, South Africa, China, Alaska, Peru, Chile (the nearest we could get to Antarctica), Easter Island, Australia, New Zealand, Hawaii, Madagascar and England, it become apparent that the experiences and understanding they brought forward facilitated healing for each traveller, the peoples and lands visited, and for humanity as a whole. It was an incredible time.

Initially, I assumed that such healing might occur as we activated the energies of the Discs by tuning in, praying and connecting energetically with our highest awareness. But we soon realized that each and every journey in its entirety was a pilgrimage of healing, with deep lessons.

Each journey had a theme that connected with the specific place we went to, its people and its history. More validation of what we were doing also came when we discovered local legends with relevant associations to the Soular Discs.

The knowledge brought forward by all the journeys offered a 12-step process for heart-centred healing, to transcend our personality-based awareness and to embody a vastly expanded perception of the Oneness of the Cosmos.

Ultimately, the pilgrimages, which also engaged with indigenous wisdom keepers around the world, were to reveal profound understanding of our human and extra-terrestrial heritage that is available to everyone. And their culmination, at the time of the astrological alignment of the Harmonic Concordance of November 2003, was guided to aid the collective shift of consciousness prophesied by many spiritual traditions.

* * * *

The completed activation of the energies of the Discs and their connection with the planetary grid support not only a shift in human awareness but for Gaia and our entire soular system too. And turning the 13th master key was ultimately revealed as the opening of a collective portal to Galactic awareness.

I believe that we are indeed in the momentous times foretold by the Mayan masters. As we travel the path towards the years 2012/2013 we may each choose to be co-creators in re-establishing relationships with Gaia and the wider Cosmos on spiritual, emotional and physical levels.

And as we do so, our awareness is expanding beyond the confines of our ego-self. By embodying our wholly inter-connected consciousness, we become resonant with an ever greater perception of the Cosmos – a homecoming to the wholeness of who we *really* are.

As I have personally discovered, if we are willing to listen, Spirit offers each of us our own unique portals to the awareness of our destiny.

For myself, and many others, the crop circles have offered one such doorway. And universal to sacred sites through-out the ages, they are microcosmic holograms of Spirit, opening our hearts, minds and purpose to a greater understanding of the world and our place within it.

Dawn Breslin

I run in the forest each day, sometimes I feel that I can touch its magical energy. I breathe it in, my soul bathes in the images that I see, the colours are incredible ... and each day they change.

I adore the cycle of life and nature. Running outside each day allows me to be part of nature. In touch with the Earth, the elements, the weather, and the wonder of the cycle of growth, birth and death – it seduces me and I feel so, so alive!

The magic of nature makes me feel humble. It reminds me that I could live in a caravan with no money, no possessions, nothing, and I would still feel so happy. It is also such a guaranteed commodity, there for each and every one of us in the form of positive energy, and it's free of charge.

There are days when I speak to the animals when I'm on my run – the way they move or communicate makes me giggle and fills my heart up with joy. Sometimes I look at a new plant emerging from the earth and I imagine it has a face – like the forest spirits. It stimulates my creativity and my mind.

Some days I open my arms up wide as I run, just to feel the wind, the sun or the rain envelop me. Other days I want to scream *'Thank you!'* for the magic I experience. I know nothing like the feeling of bathing in nature. It's not the running that gives me the high – it's nature, the colours, the sounds, the smells, the animals and the voice in my head that says that this illusion is what the magic of being human is all about. I feel blessed! I am grateful! *Gratitude at the start of the day is the key here.*

I go home into my big concrete box (which overlooks the forest) energized, fitter and refreshed, and I feel that I have lived fully *today*. What a wonderful, dramatic and energizing start to each and every day of my life.

● ●

Sally Morningstar

I hold a deep belief that life is like a mirror reflecting back to me whatever I am capable of perceiving in any given moment. I believe that this mirror is held in the hands of a loving universe, and so no matter how ugly or harsh a reflection might be, I have come to trust that there is always a wise hand behind it. Like the ancient Celts, I believe that the mirror and my soul's reflection are intricately and eternally entwined.

When things get tough, highly charged emotions can often be involved that deplete us, distract us, sometimes even nearly destroy us, and just at a time when a great deal more is being asked of us, just at a time when any ripples in the pond only serve to make it harder to see anything clearly.

Instead, I try to still any turmoil; to see clearly what is being reflected to me and to make connections. I have a close relationship with the natural world and so I turn to nature, I read the signs; I join the dots so that a clearer picture can emerge.

Thus, as I grow in wisdom and understanding, life's reflections are painted upon the magical path I have chosen to tread. To work with the mirror like this I go to the Queen of Elphame, Keeper of the Mirror of All Souls – also known as the Fairy Queen.

A MIRROR MEDITATION

The Fairy Queen holds a truly magical mirror – one that can reflect truth, guidance and clarity and also deflect harm. She carries a pure white pearl in one hand and a mirror of glass in the other. Whether or not you feel her presence, whether she remains unseen or comes in visions, dreams or through a sign (perhaps a moth, butterfly or other winged creature) we can at any time ask for her loving guidance, ask her to lead us to true reflection, or ask for her mirror to deflect away unjust negativity and protect us from harm.

There are several ways to journey to her that include sitting beneath her sacred tree, the hawthorn; upon barrows, mounds or hilltops, within caverns and grottoes or at shorelines as well as threshold places and moments (like twilight).

I begin by centring and calming myself for a few moments until I feel a magically charged atmosphere within and around me. I open my heart and soul and repeat three times:

'Mother, keeper of my soul's true light – please hear me.' (Ring a bell once after each repetition.)

I then speak about my circumstances and sometimes ask for what I feel is needed (protection, guidance, insight). In stillness, I breathe, for between 15 and 30 minutes, reflective like the surface of a mirror and open to insights. I conclude things by giving thanks and ringing a bell three times.

I then perform some act of kindness that is useful to the natural world.

Pamela J. Ball

A Perfect Gift

There have for me been several defining moments in my life which have made a profound impression. Perhaps the first that I remember was standing on the sea wall near our home in Scotland watching the tide come in. I must have been about five; it was windy and stormy and the sea was magnificent in its wildness. I remember clearly thinking that such power was exciting and frightening at the same time. I had touched something beyond understanding.

Ever since that time, both as child and adult, the sea has figured prominently in my personal imagery and indeed it is the recurrence of that original image which many years later prompted me to start researching the meaning of dreams. The sea is a representation of cosmic consciousness, a wild sea the chaos of creation, but also the breadth and depth of feminine intuition, which many have cause to fear.

As I developed clairvoyance, mediumship, dream interpretation and all the skills that I now use in my ordinary everyday life, I learned to use the power of the sea to cleanse and rejuvenate my inner being, in a way that for me might be considered nothing short of miraculous. No matter how tired or strung out I might be, good friends would often say at just the right moment, 'Fancy a day at the seaside?' and I would come back refreshed and ready to go again – to borrow a term from drug culture, I'd be quite 'high'. I remember on one particular visit, I turned a patch of sea quite dark as I let everything go. At the same time I was conscious of lifting out of my body.

At the time of the tsunami at the end of 2004, when Poseidon, the old sea-god, protested at the woeful misuse of the world's resources, all I could do was to say, 'I'm sorry,' and pour back into that vast ocean all the love, healing and caring that I could muster. Small recompense indeed for such a magnificent gift.

• •

Alberto Villoldo

We shamans have animal guides, spirit guides and angels. Your animal guides are your connection to the elemental forces of nature.

Once I was lost in the Amazon for almost four days. The first two days I told myself, 'Alberto, you're not lost. Lost is a state of mind. You simply do not know where you are.' Then after the third day, I had to admit to myself I was lost.

So I called on my power animal in the dream time and she told me to follow her tracks. The following morning, I found a set of jaguar prints and they led me, for three hours, through the Amazon, to the banks of a river. I followed them along the bank until I came to a bigger river where I found a missionary in a canoe who gave me a lift back to his house.

Nature makes me happiest of all. Hiking along the Andes mountains is my favourite pastime. Machu Picchu is one particularly special place where I've spent many nights meditating under the stars. After a while, I became addicted to the incredible revelations I was having. But I discovered that they were a temporary euphoria and it's the moment-by-moment feeling of being alive that is the gift. Every moment should be cherished, not just those moments of epiphany and revelation, which in a way were distracting from the real beauty of the everyday.

My meditations are about being in a deep quiet place and then seeing the kind of world that I want my children's children to inherit. I'm not interested in fixing little problems, one at a time. Let's dream about how all the world could be, where people live in peace with each other, where the rivers are clean, where the air is pure.

Glennie Kindred

Diary

Walking meditation has become my new pleasure in life. It has all the benefits of the more usual sitting meditation but also gives me a deeper communion with my environment. I make a conscious decision to keep my focus on my breathing in the usual way, gently acknowledging my thoughts but not encouraging them. And I create stillness within me. I kindle Love, Compassion and Delight for the world around me.

I walk in meditation in many different places and situations, but my favourite is to walk in the woods. I keep a journal to record my insights and understanding that come from these meditation walks. This is one such entry.

> I am in the silent winter woods again, drawn here by my need to be alone, to be close to the Earth and the trees. A sense of stillness touches me as I walk amongst the trees and I become conscious that I have slipped into their energy field. I respond to this by slowing down and a wonderful calmness comes over me. I breathe deeply, taking in the oxygen-rich air, laden with life-giving molecules, the precious unseen gift from the trees. I am aware that as I breathe in these organic compounds, they are becoming part of me as they enter inside my lungs and then are absorbed into my bloodstream. I am literally breathing

in the essence of the trees.

I send my gratitude to the trees. Their great gifts of healing are simply and freely given to all. We have only to sit with them and breathe with them to feel the benefits.

Today I am drawn to sit with an oak tree which stands on a raised hillock surrounded by young silver birch, and as I sit with my back to its trunk, I look out over the valley below and sense the deep stability of being rooted to this one spot. I give myself time to sit and daydream and wait to see what inspiration comes.

The secret of communicating with trees lies in our ability to slow down enough to register how the trees are communicating with us. This is their great gift to us, for it requires a shift in our perception. Trees don't talk to us with words, trees communicate in energy-images, which trigger our emotional response. This is an older form of communication than language, and to experience it I must learn how to move into the stillness within me, to experience that elusive interface that lies at the edge of Time. In Celtic mythology it is called the 'Place Between the Worlds' or the 'Otherworld', the interface between our surface reality and Spirit, a place of magic and mystery.

The unity and completeness of this tree is reflected back to me and I experience a shift in understanding that triggers a new awareness of myself. It is this that I seek in the stillness of the winter woods, this experience of Oneness with all of life, knowing that I am so much more than my surface reality.

Here, in the dark of the year, when the days are short and the Earth is still, I rest, and in the stillness become aware of new seeds that are forming within me, new parts of myself waiting to grow when the time is right.

I ask myself , 'What do I wish to bring into my life? What do I wish to grow within myself?' These are my seeds of transformation, my seeds of hope and seeds of the future. What I change in myself is reflected out into my life and adds to the change in the world.

We are all responsible for the world we create. I envision a growing number of people who make the move from the old view of separation and domination to a new inclusive Unity and respect for the Earth, each other and the whole integrated web of all life.

CONTRIBUTORS DIRECTORY

Jane Alexander
Books include *The Detox Kit* (Hay House), *The Overload Solution* (Piatkus) and *Spirit of the Home* (Thorsons).
Go to www.janealexander.org for more information.

Caroline Shola Arewa
Books include *Opening to Spirit*, *Way of the Chakras* (both Thorsons) and *Embracing Purpose, Passion and Peace* (Inner Vision Books).
For more details go to www.creatingease.com, www.success-withoutstress.net or email shola@creatingease.com.

Pamela J. Ball
Books include *The Complete Book of Dreams and Dreaming*, *10,000 Ways to Change Your Life* (both Arcturus) and *A Woman's Way to Wisdom* (Quantum).

Barefoot Doctor
Books include *Handbook for the Urban Warrior* (Piatkus), *Liberation* and *Manifesto* (both Thorsons).
Visit www.barefootdoctorworld.co.uk.

Sarah Bartlett
Books include *Fated Attraction* (HarperCollins), *Women, Sex and Astrology* and *Feng Shui for Lovers* (both Orion).
See www.sarahbartlett.com for more details or, for consultations and correspondence, email sarah@sarahbartlett.com.

Brian Bates

Books include the international bestseller *The Way of Wyrd* (Hay House).

Go to www.wayofwyrd.com and www.brianbates.co.uk for more information.

Laura Berridge

Runs workshops and consultations called Rediscover & Dress the Goddess Within You to help clients dress in a way that expresses their essence.

Go to www.goddesscollection.co.uk for more details.

William Bloom

Books include *The Endorphin Effect, Working with Angels, Feeling Safe* and *Psychic Protection* (all Piatkus) – and most recently *Soulution: The Holistic Manifesto (*Hay House).

See www.holism.info for more details on holism, and go to www.williambloom.com for more information or email wm@williambloom.com.

Dawn Breslin

Books include *Zest for Life* and *The Power Book* (both Hay House).

Go to www.dawnbreslin.com for more information.

Dr John Briffa

Books include *Ultimate Health – 12 Keys to Abundant Health and Happiness* (Penguin) and *Natural Health for Kids* (Michael Joseph).

Visit www.drbriffa.com for more.

Simon Brown

Books include *The Practical Art of Face Reading* (Carroll & Brown) and *Feng Shui Bible* (Godfield Press). A member of the Feng Shui Society, Macrobiotic Association and Shiatsu Society. Call 020 7431 9897, email simon@chienergy.co.uk or visit www.chienergy.co.uk for more details.

Deepak Chopra, MD

Bestsellers include *Ageless Body, Timeless Mind* (Rider & Co.); *The Seven Spiritual Laws of Success* (Excel Books), *Grow Younger, Live Longer: 10 Steps to Reverse Aging* and *The Path to Love* (both Rider & Co.).

Go to www.chopra.com for more details.

Sonia Choquette

Books include *Vitamins for the Soul* and *Trust Your Vibes* (both Hay House).

Go to www.soniachoquette.com for more details.

Carina Coen

In her Mercarina therapy business, she is constantly exploring the concept of merging creative, holistic and beauty therapies and ideas for ultimate wellbeing.

For more information go to www.mercarina.com.

Diana Cooper

Books include *Angel Inspiration, Discover Atlantis* and her spiritual fiction series (all Hodder Mobius), plus many angel oracle cards and meditation CDs.

Go to www.dianacooper.com for more information.

Hazel Courteney

Books include three health books, two cookery books and two spiritual books, plus *The Evidence for the Sixth Sense* (Cico Books).

Log on to www.hazelcourteney.com for more details.

Jude Currivan, PhD

Books include books include *The Wave* (O Books), *The 8th Chakra* (Hay House), and *Many Voices, One Heart* (out soon from Hay House).

For more information visit www.judecurrivan.com.

Sarah Dening

Books include *The Everyday I Ching* (Simon & Schuster); *The Mythology of Sex* (BT Batsford) and *Healing Dreams* (Hamlyn).

See more on her website, www.sarahdening.net.

Dronma

Her artwork and more information can be seen on www.dronma-art.com.

Dr Wayne W. Dyer

Books include *Secrets of Your Own Healing Power, Wisdom of the Masters* and *The Power of Intention* (all Hay House).

Visit www.drwaynedyer.com for more details.

Cassandra Eason

Books on magic, divination, psychic development and nature spirituality include *Cassandra Eason's Complete Book of Tarot* and *Cassandra's Psychic Party Games* (both Piatkus).

Go to www.cassandraeason.co.uk for more information.

Chris Fleming

Presenter and paranormal investigator on Living TV's *Dead Famous*.

Visit www.unknownmagazine.com for more news.

Lynne Franks

Books include *The SEED Handbook: the Feminine Way to Create Business* and *GROW* and *The Modern Woman's Handbook* (both Hay House).

See www.lynnefranks.com for more details.

Adam Fronteras

Books include *Instant Tarot* (Collins & Brown) and *Family Sun Signs* (Zambezi Publishing). He also runs Esoteric Entertainment Company, which specializes in providing psychic content for the media.

Go to www.adamfronteras.co.uk for more information.

George David Fryer

Regularly works with and holds workshops with medium Samatha Hamilton.

For more information and artwork of spirit guides visit www.georgedavidfryer.co.uk.

Alicen Geddes-Ward

Books include *Faeriecraft* (Hay House). Alicen holds work-shops around the UK. Go to www.faeriecraft.co.uk for more details.

Samantha Hamilton

For more details on her workshops, retreats and readings go to www.mettacentre.co.uk.

Joan Hanger

Books include *Diana's Dreams* (Blake Publishing) and *The Little Book of Dreams* (Penguin). Contact her via www.penguin.co.uk.

Hamilton Harris

For more information email Hamilton on hharris391@btinternet.com or call 0207 928 7733.

Fiona Harrold

Books include the bestselling *Be Your Own Life Coach*, *Ten Minute Life Coach* and her latest, *The Seven Rules of Success* (all Hodder Mobius).
For futher information go to www.fionaharrold.com.

Louise L. Hay

Books include *Heal Your Body* and *You Can Heal Your Life* (both Hay House). Visit www.louisehay.com for more information.

Tracy Higgs

Tracy runs a psychic development circle, holds workshops and is available for private readings.
For more information email
spiritpsychiccentre@hotmail.co.uk or call 0870 757 0690.

Inbaal

Catch Inbaal giving readings on TV or writing in the press.
Visit www.inbaal.com for more information.

Judi James

Books include six novels and eight non-fiction books on body language, self-motivation and stress management.
For more information go to www.judijames.com.

Dadi Janki

Books include *Companion of God* (Hodder) and many works for the BKWSU.
For more details visit www.bkwsu.org.

Pauline Kennedy

For more details, plus private shamanic healing and Feng Shui consultations, go to www.mightyspirit.com.

Glennie Kindred

Books include nine on celebrating the Celtic festivals, herb lore, hedgerow food, tree lore, the Celtic Tree Ogham, the five elements, and her latest, *The Alchemist's Journey* (Hay House).
For more information contact her on glenniekindred@w3z.co.uk.

Michele Knight

Michele does personal readings, holds workshops and writes articles for the national press.
Visit www.micheleknight.co.uk or call 020 7497 2423 for details.

Lucy Lam

For astro queries and readings, contact lucylamastro@yahoo.co.uk

Stephen Langley

Catch Stephen lecturing around the world on naturopathic medicine and running a busy health practice at the Hale Clinic in London.
Contact him at the Hale Clinic on 020 7631 0156.

Richard Lawrence

Books include *Realise Your Inner Potential* (Aetherius Press).
For more details on Richard's meditation centre see
www.innerpotential.org. For more information on the man
himself please visit www.richardlawrence.co.uk.

Gina Lazenby

Books include *The Feng Shui House Book* and *The Healthy
Home* (both Conran Octopus).
Go to www.thehealthyhome.com for more information.

Leora Lightwoman

Author of *Tantra: The Path to Blissful Sex* (Piatkus).
For more information visit www.diamondlighttantra.com or
call 08700 780 584.

Robin Lown

Catch Robin expertly reading palms in the press, on TV and
on stage.
For consultations call 01424 731 895.

Mandy Masters

For more information on her demonstrations and shows, and
for personal readings, go to www.mandymasters.com, call
01375 402 061 or email info@mandymasters.com.

Sue Minns

Author of *Soulmates: Understanding the True Nature of Intense
Encounters* (Hodder Mobius).
She can be contacted by email on minns6@aol.com or by
telephone on 01803 863 656.

Sally Morningstar

Books include *The Art of Wiccan Healing* (Hay House), *The Wiccan Way* (Walking Stick Press) and *The Wicca Pack* (Godsfield Press).

Go to www.sallymorningstar.com for more information.

Leon Nacson

Author of nine books including three bestselling dreams books (Hay House).

See www.dreamcoach.com.au for details.

Michael Neill

Author of *You Can Have What You Want* (Hay House).

Visit him online at www.geniuscatalyst.com.

Kelfin Oberon

Self-published four collections of poems called *Accelerating Rhymes* including *The Return of Da Faeries*, and produces a regular newsletter also called Accelerating Times.

Enquiries welcome; contact kelfinoberon@hotmail.com.

Dr Susan Phoenix

Books include *Out of the Shadows: A Journey Back from Grief* (Hodder Mobius) and her forthcoming book, *Angels, Auras and Energies*.

See www.phoenixplanes.com for more details.

Penney Poyzer

Presenter of *No Waste Like Home* and author of the book of the same name.

See www.msarch.co.uk/ecohome/ for details of Penney's own eco-home. For more information on Penney herself go to www.nci-management.com.

Emma Restall Orr

Books include *Living Druidry* (Piatkus) and *Druid Priestess* (HarperCollins). She has appeared many times on television, radio and in the press as an author of Druidry.

For more information go to www.druidnetwork.org.

Jon Sandifer

Books include *Macrobiotics for Beginners* and *Feng Shui* (both Piatkus).

Visit www.fengshui.co.uk for further information on Jon's books, courses and advice.

Ian John Shillito

Co-author of forthcoming book *Behind the Curtain: West End Theatre Ghosts Revealed.*

For more details go to www.theglitterkeepsonfalling.org.uk.

Sarah Shurety

Books including *Quick Feng Shui Cures* and *Feng Shui for Your Home* (both Rider & Co.).

Visit www.fengshuisite.com for more information, books and products.

Silja

For more details, spell advice and information on witchcraft email silja@iamawitch.com.

Gordon Smith

Books include *Spirit Messenger, The Unbelievable Truth, Through My Eyes* and *Stories from the Other Side* (all Hay House).

For more information go to www.psychicbarber.co.uk.

Chuck Spezzano
Author of *Happiness is the Best Revenge* and *If It Hurts, It Isn't Love* (Hodder Mobius) and creator of the breakthrough therapeutic healing model Psychology of Vision.
Go to www.psychologyofvision.com for details.

Shelley von Strunckel
Her columns in publications around the world are read in six languages. These can also be accessed on her website www.shelleyvonstrunckel.com.

Alla Svirinskaya
Author of *Energy Secrets* (Hay House) and has appeared many times on television, radio and in the press.
For further details visit www.allasvirinskaya.com.

Angela Tarry
For more information on aura photography, colour healing and private consultations, email AngelaTarry@aol.com.

Gloria Thomas
Author of six books, the latest being *Anxiety Tool Box* (Thorsens Element).
For more details see www.reshape.co.uk.

Eckhart Tolle
Author of the bestselling book *The Power of Now*, followed by *Stillness Speaks* (both Hodder Mobius) and his latest *A New Earth* (Penguin).
Go to www.eckharttolle.com for more information.

Alberto Villoldo
Books include *Mending the Past, Healing the Future with Soul Retrieval* and *Shaman, Healer, Sage* (both Hay House).
Visit www.thefourwinds.com for more details.

Doreen Virtue
Author of more than 20 books about angels, chakras, Crystal Children, Indigo Children, health and diet, including the best-selling *Healing with the Angels* and *Messages from Your Angels* books and angel oracle cards (all Hay House).
For more details go to www.angeltherapy.com.

Jayne Wallace
For more information on readings go to www.jaynewallace.co.uk or email jayne@jaynewallace.co.uk.

Becky Walsh
Co-author of the forthcoming books *Behind the Curtain: West End Theatre Ghosts Revealed* and *Acting with Spirit: Change your life dramatically*!
Go to www.lightofspirit.com for more details of workshops and events.

Summer Watson
For details on house healing and consultations, email summer-awatson@yahoo.co.uk or call 01249 712 296.

Wyatt Webb
Books include *Five Steps to Overcoming Fear and Self-Doubt, It's Not About The Horse* and *What To Do When You Don't Know What To Do* (all Hay House). Go to www.miravalresort.com for more details.

David Wells

Auhtor of forthcoming book *David Wells' Complete Guide to Developing Your Psychic Skills* (Hay House).

Go to www.davidwells.co.uk for more news and information on his appearances on Living TV's *Most Haunted* and other television shows.

Kate West

Author of *The Real Witches' Handbook* and others in *The Real Witches' …* series (HarperCollins), amongst others.

Visit www.pyewacket.demon.co.uk to find out more.

Stuart Wilde

Author of 15 books on consciousness and awareness, including *Life Was Never Meant to Be a Struggle*, *Silent Power* and *God's Gladiators* (all Hay House). Go to www.stuartwilde.com for more information.

Perry Wood

Author of *Secrets of the People Whisperer* (Rider & Co).

For more information, visit www.peoplewhisperer.com.

Hay House Titles of Related Interest

The Four Insights: Wisdom, Power and Grace of the Earthkeepers,
by Alberto Villodo PhD

You Can Have What You Want, by Michael Neill

Faeriecraft, by Alicen and Neil Geddes-Ward

How to Develop Your Psychic Skills,
by David Wells

Energy Secrets: The Ultimate Well-Being Plan,
by Alla Svirinskaya

Through My Eyes, by Gordon Smith

Stories from the Other Side, by Gordon Smith

*The SEED Handbook: The Feminine Way to
Create Business,* by Lynne Franks

Dawn Breslin's Power Book, by Dawn Breslin

*Soulution: How Today's Spirituality Changes
Everything,* by William Bloom

The Way of Wyrd, by Brian Bates

Diary of a Psychic: Shattering the Myth,
by Sonia Choquette

Inspiration: Your Ultimate Calling,
by Dr Wayne W. Dyer

The Power of Intention, by Dr Wayne W. Dyer

Goddesses & Angels: Awaken Your Inner High-Priestess and Source-eress, by Doreen Virtue PhD

Healing with the Angels: How the Angels Can Assist You in Every Area of Your Life, by Doreen Virtue PhD

Messages from Your Angels Oracle Cards, by Doreen Virtue PhD

The Lightworker's Way: Awakening Your Spiritual Power to Know and Heal, by Doreen Virtue PhD

You Can Heal Your Life, by Louise L. Hay

Heal Your Body, by Louise L. Hay

Meditations to Heal Your Life, by Louise L. Hay

The 8th Chakra, by Jude Currivan

The Art of Wiccan Healing, by Sally Morningstar

Earth Wisdom, by Glennie Kindred

SPIRIT&DESTINY

Discover more Soul Secrets inside the pages of
Spirit & Destiny magazine.

Every issue will help you find out more about the worlds of
astrology, psychics and holistic therapies. You will be
entertained by absorbing features on everything from angels to
feng shui and alternative lifestyles, and gain a fascinating insight
into your future, your personality, life and relationships.

Spirit & Destiny magazine is available every month at your
local newsagents or supermarket.

Exclusive Offer

Subscribe and Save 30%!

As a *Soul Secrets* reader we are delighted to give you & your
friends a fantastic opportunity subscribe to *Spirit & Destiny*
magazine for only £24.00.

That's 12 issues delivered to your door,
saving you an amazing £10.80!

Call us today to take advantage of this fantastic offer.
Simply quote 'Soul Secrets' to save 30%.

ORDER HOTLINE 01795-414847
(Monday-Friday 9am-5.30pm)
Or you can email us at **spirit@galleon.co.uk**

We hope you enjoyed this Hay House book.
If you would like to receive a free catalogue featuring additional
Hay House books and products, or if you would like information
about the Hay Foundation, please contact:

Hay House UK Ltd
292B Kensal Rd • London W10 5BE
Tel: (44) 20 8962 1230; Fax: (44) 20 8962 1239
www.hayhouse.co.uk

***

Published and distributed in the United States of America by:
Hay House, Inc. • PO Box 5100 • Carlsbad, CA 92018-5100
Tel: (1) 760 431 7695 or (800) 654 5126;
Fax: (1) 760 431 6948 or (800) 650 5115
www.hayhouse.com

Published and distributed in Australia by:
Hay House Australia Ltd • 18/36 Ralph St • Alexandria NSW 2015
Tel: (61) 2 9669 4299; Fax: (61) 2 9669 4144
www.hayhouse.com.au

Published and distributed in the Republic of South Africa by:
Hay House SA (Pty) Ltd • PO Box 990 • Witkoppen 2068
Tel/Fax: (27) 11 706 6612 • orders@psdprom.co.za

Distributed in Canada by:
Raincoast • 9050 Shaughnessy St • Vancouver, BC V6P 6E5
Tel: (1) 604 323 7100; Fax: (1) 604 323 2600

***

Sign up via the Hay House UK website to receive the Hay House
online newsletter and stay informed about what's going on with
your favourite authors. You'll receive bimonthly announcements
about discounts and offers, special events, product highlights,
free excerpts, giveaways, and more!
www.hayhouse.co.uk